BPMN Process Exam|

Modelling Business Processes Using Practical Examples

Kenneth J Sherry

First Published 2015

By Admaks Publishing

www.admaks.com

First edition 2015

Table of Contents

Introduction

BPMN is an established and extensive business process notation providing many ways to diagrammatically define solutions. After receiving many requests to demonstrate the use of BPMN, I decided to modify some of my past business process models and collate them into BPMN Process Examples.

The book comprises of six complete examples of end to end business process models and shows alternative modelling techniques.

Each example has an overview, the choreography between the collaborating partners and the BPD of the inline sub-processes.

The sub-processes are shown in separate BPD's depicting the tasks needed to complete the inline process.

The book pages are designed so that the description is on the left side of the page and the BDP on the right, allowing the reader to view the description and the BDP at the same time.

Process 1	Handle Incoming Post

About the process

This example describes a simple post room process to handle the incoming post and could apply to small to medium sized companies.

A post room database is used and partitioned by department, with each department having its own access rights.

The arriving post is scanned and stored in the appropriate departmental partition of the post room database, enabling each department to access their post directly online.

Process collaboration

The Handle Incoming Post Process has three pools; the incoming post room with the sub-processes, the multi-instance black box pool which describes the process of each department and a black box pool describing the national post.

Overview:	Handle Incoming Post Process

1. The post arrives at 9:00 and 16:00 every working day
2. The post is first sorted and put into pigeon holes
3. Confidential post is not opened but envelopes are registered and scanned
4. Non-confidential post is registered, scanned and archived
5. Emails are sent to departments to inform them that post is available on the post database
6. Emails are sent to employees to inform them that personal letters are available for collection from the post room
7. Confidential post is delivered to the respective departments
8. All department post is archived in a paper filing system
9. The HR, Finance and Procurement post is delivered to the respective departments

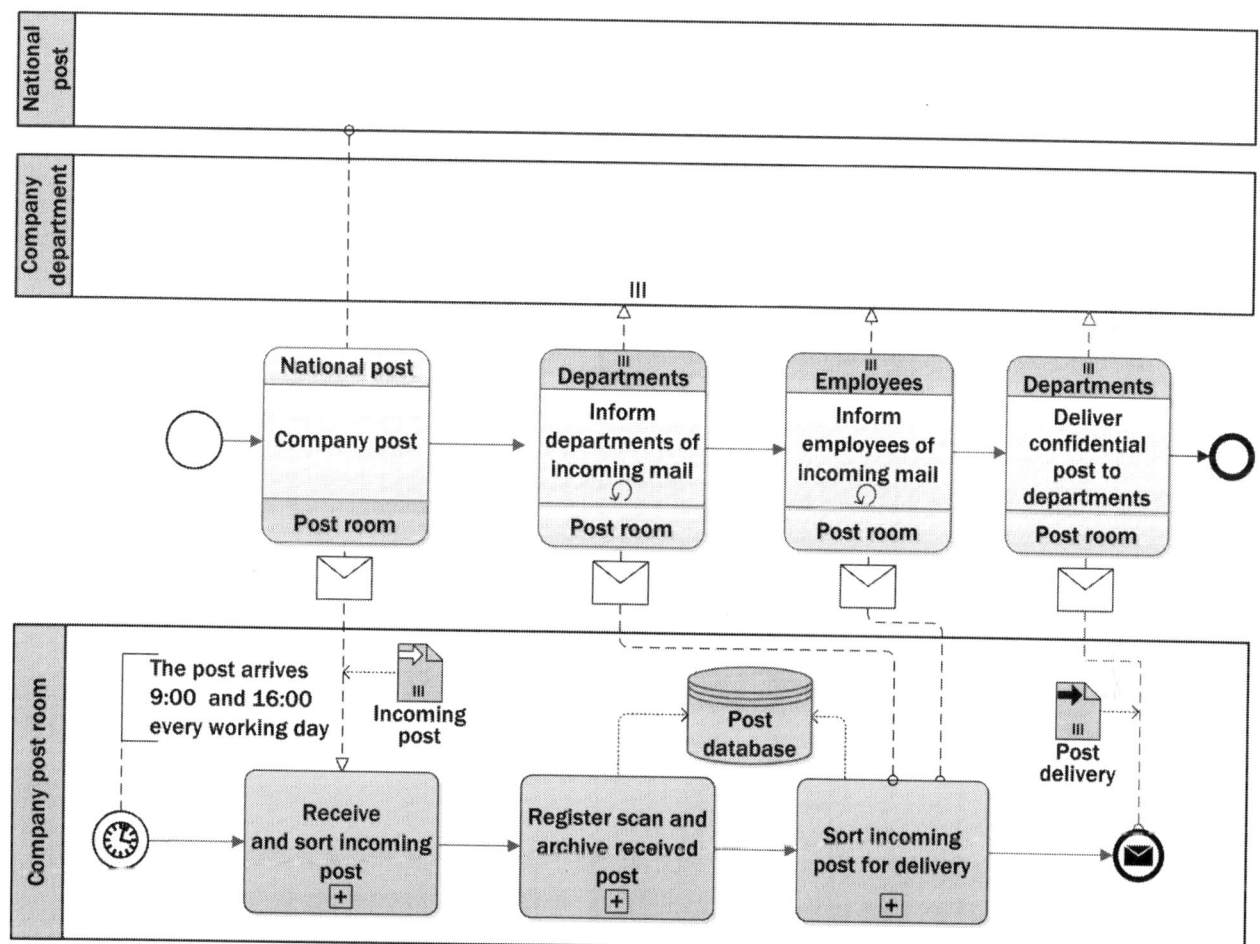

Sub-process: Receive And Sort Incoming Post

1. The incoming post arrives

2. Post recipients are checked

3. Post is sorted into departments

4. If envelopes are confidential, they are not opened but placed in the appropriate pigeon hole

5. If envelopes are non-confidential, they are opened and placed in the appropriate pigeon hole

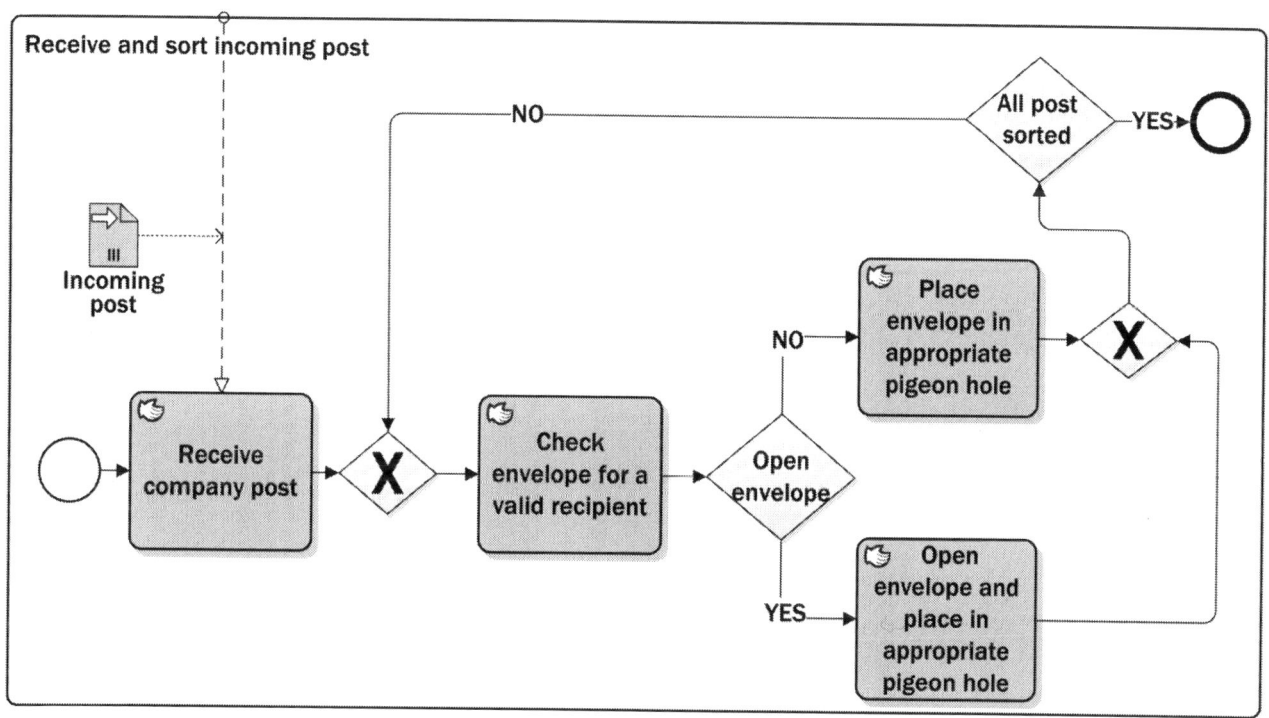

Receive and sort incoming post

- Incoming post
- Receive company post
- Check envelope for a valid recipient
- Open envelope
  - NO → Place envelope in appropriate pigeon hole
  - YES → Open envelope and place in appropriate pigeon hole
- All post sorted
  - NO
  - YES

Sub-process:	Register Departmental Post And Scan

1. Registration labels are printed with a serial number

2. Post from each department pigeon hole is retrieved and the registration label is attached to either the envelope or the letter

3. All letters are scanned into the post database

4. Non opened envelopes are scanned into the post database

5. Post to be delivered is returned to the pigeon holes

6. Non-confidential post is collated into a monthly file

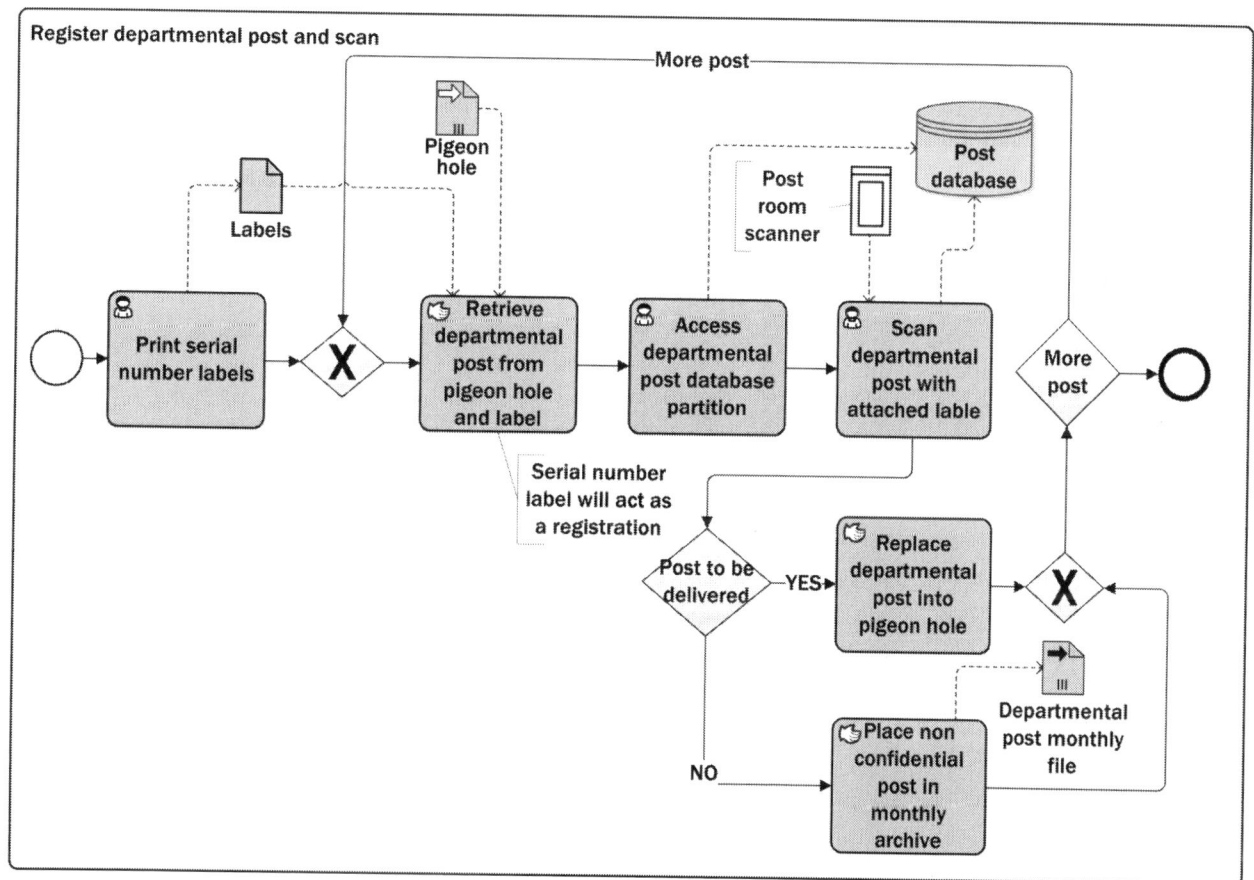

Register departmental post and scan

- More post
- Labels
- Pigeon hole
- Print serial number labels
- Retrieve departmental post from pigeon hole and label
- Access departmental post database partition
- Post room scanner
- Post database
- Scan departmental post with attached lable
- More post
- Serial number label will act as a registration
- Post to be delivered
- YES — Replace departmental post into pigeon hole
- NO — Place non confidential post in monthly archive
- Departmental post monthly file

Sub-process:	Sort Incoming Post For Delivery

1. Each department is informed by email, that letters have arrived and are available on the post database

2. Employees are sent an email that private letters have arrived and are ready to be collected from the post room

3. Private post is placed in the appropriate out tray

4. Confidential post is collated into the respective departments

5. The post trolley is then prepared with specific post

Admaks Publishing - BPMN Process Examples

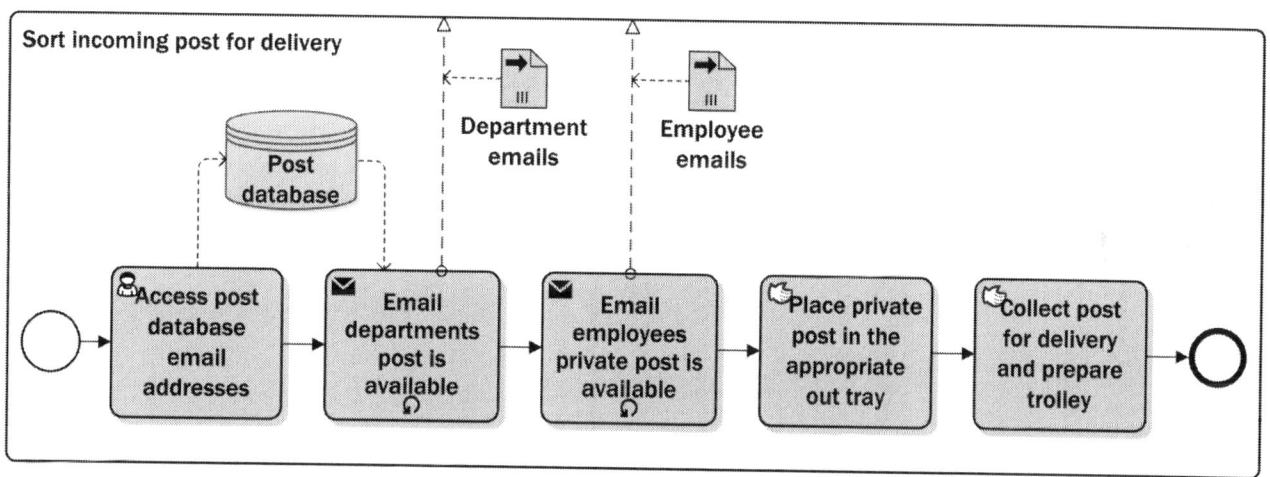

Sort incoming post for delivery

Post database

Department emails

Employee emails

Access post database email addresses

Email departments post is available

Email employees private post is available

Place private post in the appropriate out tray

Collect post for delivery and prepare trolley

Process 1 Alternative Modelling Techniques

1.1   The inline process is depicted with a timer start event, as the message flow goes directly into **Receive and sort incoming post** sub-process. In this instance a none start event would be sufficient. The **Receive and sort incoming post** sub-process could then be depicted as a Receive task initiating a process.

1.2   A post room scanner artefact is depicted although BPMN does not stipulate the use of these artefacts. However, it is not necessary to use this artefact as the task describes the activity.

1.3   A printer artefact could be used to describe the output of the **Print serial number labels** task.

1.4   The **Inform departments of incoming post** choreography task, could have a reply message to confirm the department has been informed at a specific time/date.

Process 2	Handle Outgoing Post

About the process

This example describes a simple post room process handling outgoing post. It could apply to small to medium sized companies. During the working day, outgoing non-confidential letters are stored on the post database by employees.

Confidential letters are handed over to the post room in an envelope ready for franking. Private letters are delivered to the post room already stamped.

When incoming post is delivered by the post room staff to HR, Finance and Procurement, any outgoing confidential post is collected. Any post is given to the national post when the post is received.

Process collaboration

The **Outgoing Post** process collaborates with each department only through the post database and a black box describing the national post.

Overview:	**Outgoing Post Process**

1. Company non-confidential outgoing letters are saved on the post database and subsequently printed by the post room staff before post is collected
2. Letters are sealed and franked ready for collection
3. Confidential letters are delivered to the post room already sealed and then franked by the post room before being collected by the national post
4. An hour before the national post collection, non confidential letters from each department are printed, put in envelopes and franked
5. Employees deliver their own private letters ready for posting

Admaks Publishing - BPMN Process Examples

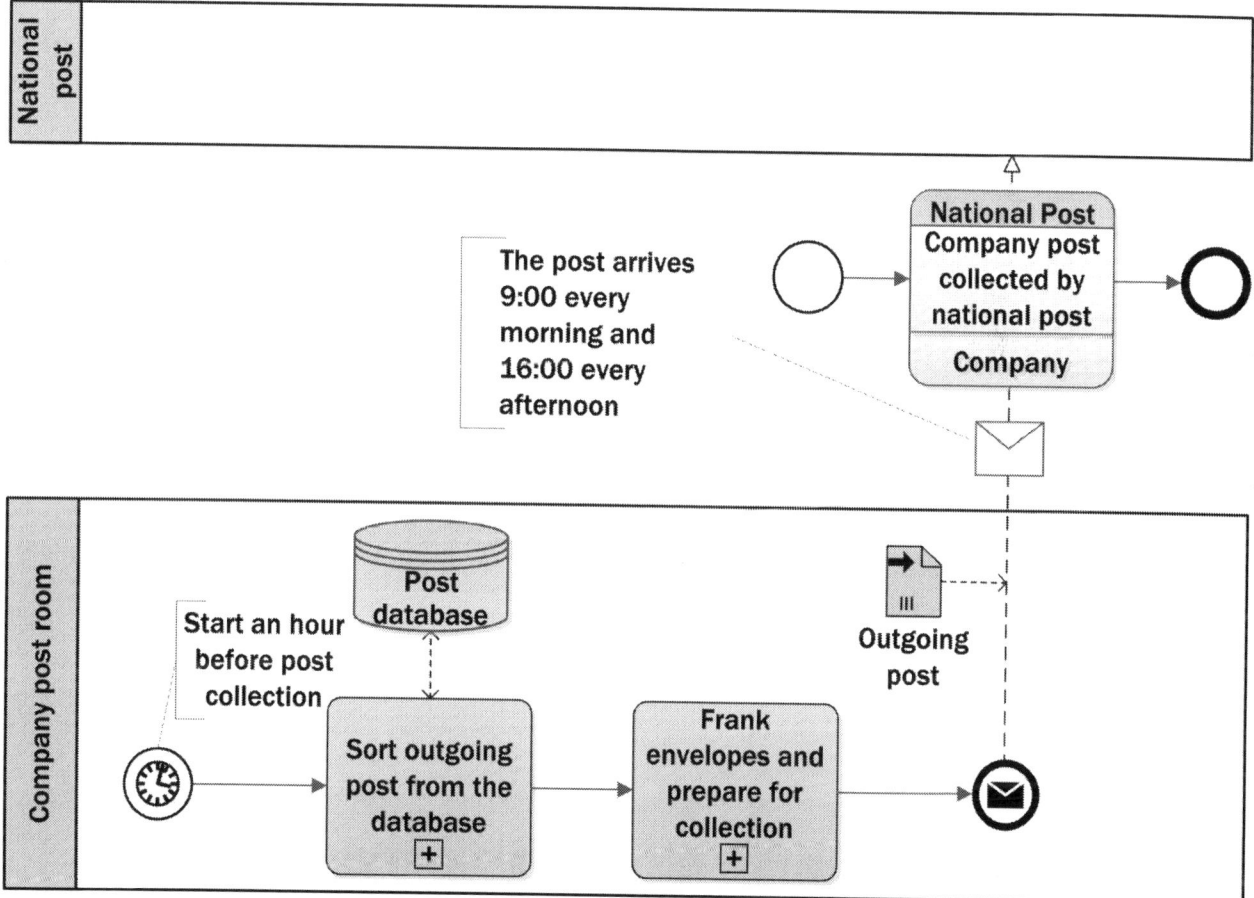

National post

The post arrives 9:00 every morning and 16:00 every afternoon

National Post
Company post collected by national post
Company

Company post room

Post database

Start an hour before post collection

Sort outgoing post from the database

Frank envelopes and prepare for collection

Outgoing post

Sub-process: Sort Outgoing Post From The Database

1. Access post database for outgoing post

2. Select specific letter type

3. Print letter from the database

4. Check if envelope is required to have a printed address label

5. Insert letter into envelope

6. Place letter in the out tray

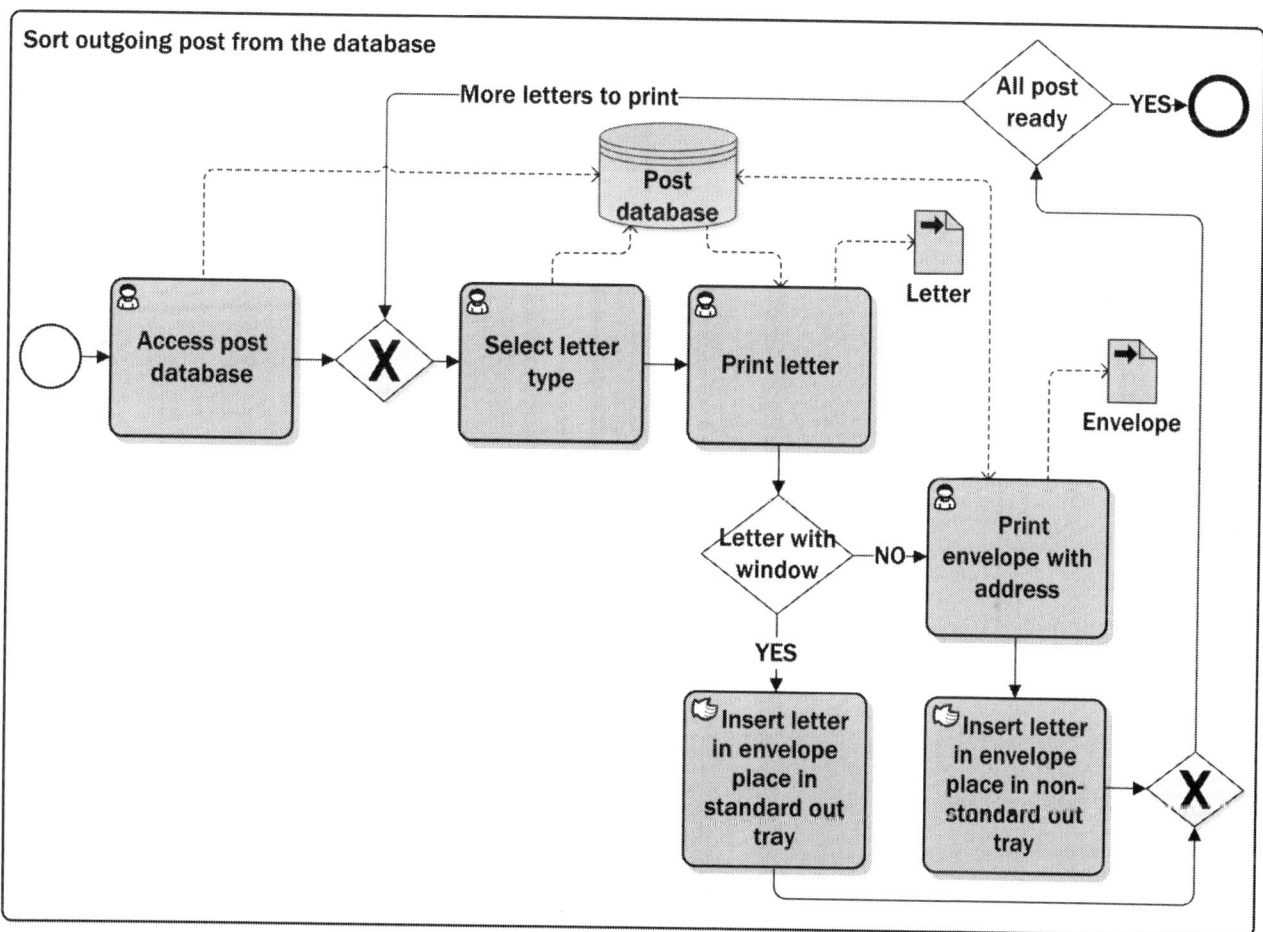

Sort outgoing post from the database

- More letters to print
- All post ready — YES
- Access post database
- X
- Select letter type
- Print letter
- Letter
- Post database
- Envelope
- Letter with window — NO → Print envelope with address
- YES
- Insert letter in envelope place in standard out tray
- Insert letter in envelope place in non-standard out tray
- X

Sub-process:	Frank Envelopes And Prepare For Collection

1. Retrieve standard post and frank the envelopes

2. Retrieve non-standard post and frank the envelopes

3. Assemble post ready for collection

4. The national post arrives

5. The outgoing post is handed over

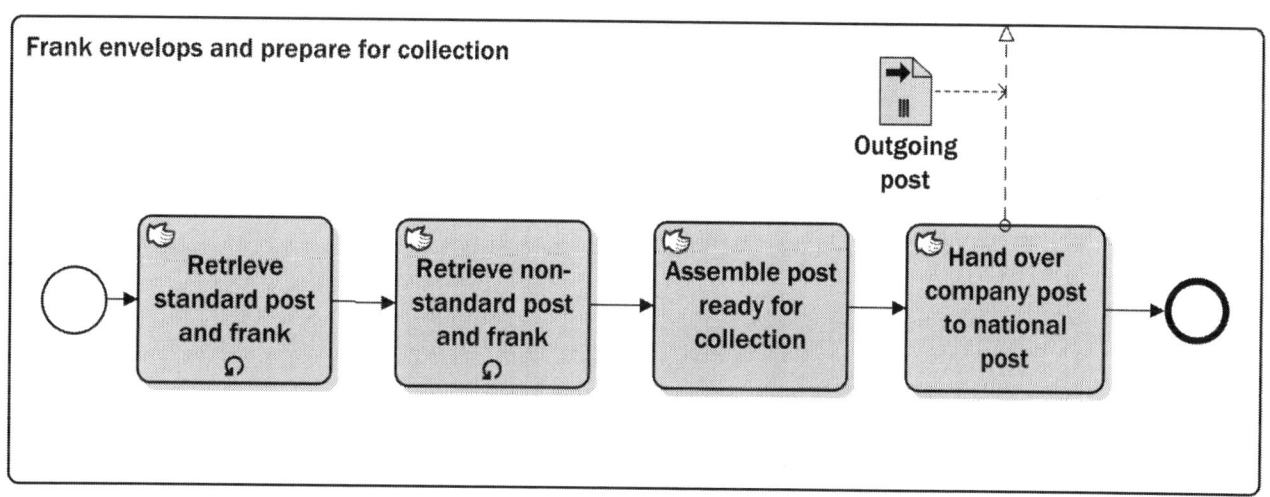

Frank envelops and prepare for collection

Outgoing post

Retrieve standard post and frank

Retrieve non-standard post and frank

Assemble post ready for collection

Hand over company post to national post

Process 2 Alternative Modelling Techniques

2.1   The inline process is depicted with a timer start event and with the annotation **Start an hour before post collection**. As the time of collection is not always the same and the number of letters is not known, an alternative could be a specific time to start the process. This would allow sufficient time to print all the post.

2.2   The letters and envelopes could be printed for each department at one time, although the type of envelope will differ with the letter types.

2.3   A franking machine artefact could be depicted which would then change the manual task to a user task.

Admaks Publishing - BPMN Process Examples

Process 3   Furniture Direct

About the process

Furniture Direct is one of the business processes of a furniture company. The business process starts when an order is received for furniture products. The customer is sent an order confirmation. Products from stock are delivered within 15 working days from order. Any unavailable parts are ordered. A delivery schedule is sent to the customer. The warehouse is informed when products are available. Products are packed and shipped. The Finance Department Process is required to respond and advise on customer credit worthiness.

Process Collaboration

The Furniture Direct process collaborates with three separate participants. The Customer process which orders the products and awaits confirmation, the Parts Supplier process which is used when parts are required and the Shipping Company process which receives the order to deliver the products.

Furniture Direct business Process

1. The **Customer** sends an order to the Back Office of the Furniture Company which checks and sends confirmation to the customer

2. The customer requirements are sent to the **Assemble** department which checks the order and if parts are unavailable, sends an order to **Parts supplier**

3. The **Parts supplier** process will not always be needed therefore the choreography sequence will be re-directed, when parts are not required

4. Assemble Department sends a delivery schedule to the customer

5. Products are assembled when parts are available

6. When products are ready, the completed work order is sent to the Back Office for an invoice and delivery note

7. Products are sent to the Warehouse for shipping and a dialogue is started to find the **Shipping company** with the best ETA and cost

8. The request for cost and ETA message will be sent to several Shipping Companies, therefore the **Shipping company** pool is depicted as a multi-instance pool

9. Products are delivered to the customer by the selected shipping company

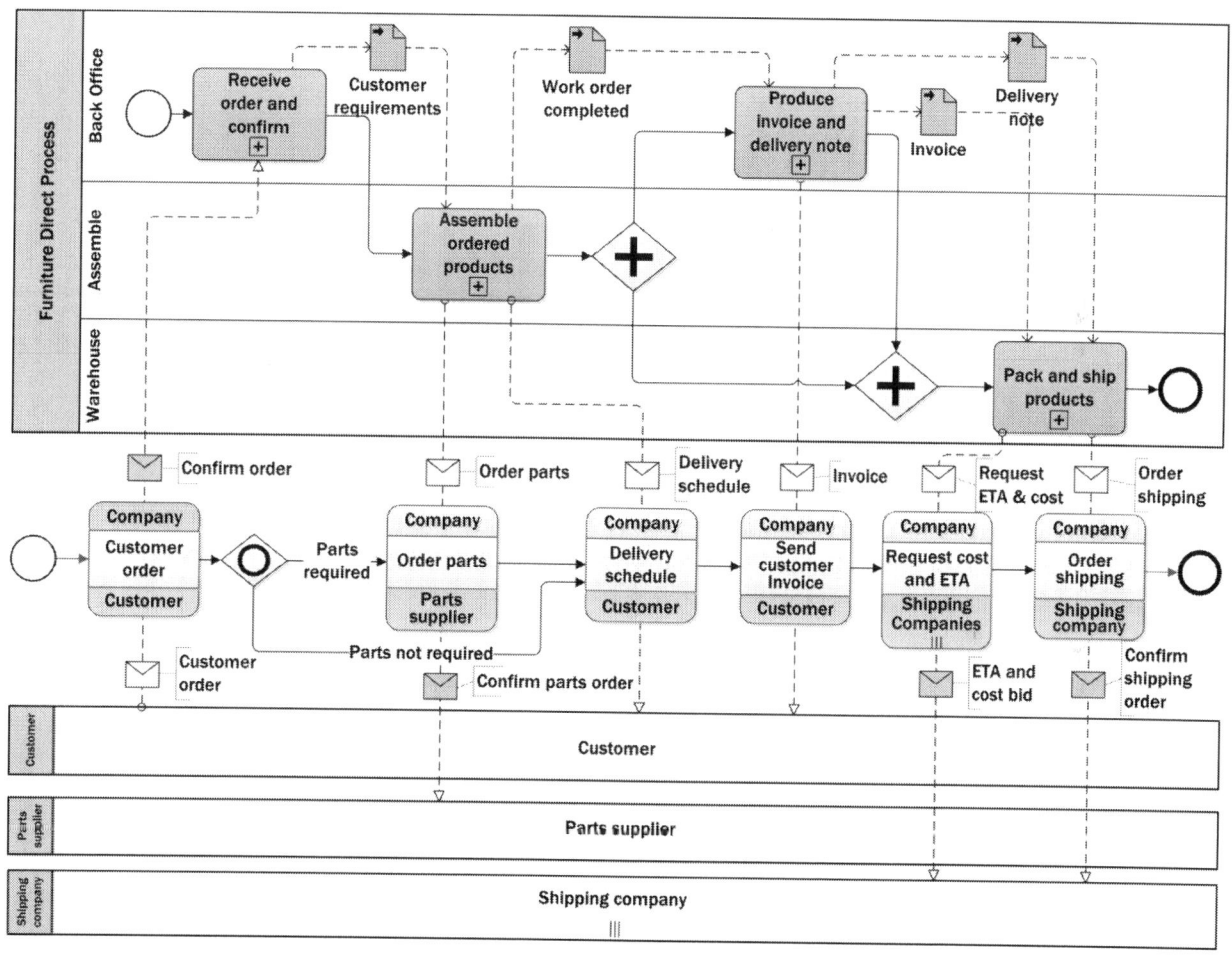

Sub-process:	**Receive Order And Confirm**

1. The order is received and the customer is checked on the database

2. New customers are entered in the database

3. The customer is checked for credit worthiness

4. If the credit check is positive, the order is processed and conformation is sent to the customer

5. If the credit check is questionable, finance will advise whether to proceed with the order. If allowed to proceed, an order conformation is sent to the customer with a request for COD

6. If customer credit is negative, the order is not processed and an Unable to Complete Order is sent to the customer

7. If the order is to proceed, a requirements list is produced

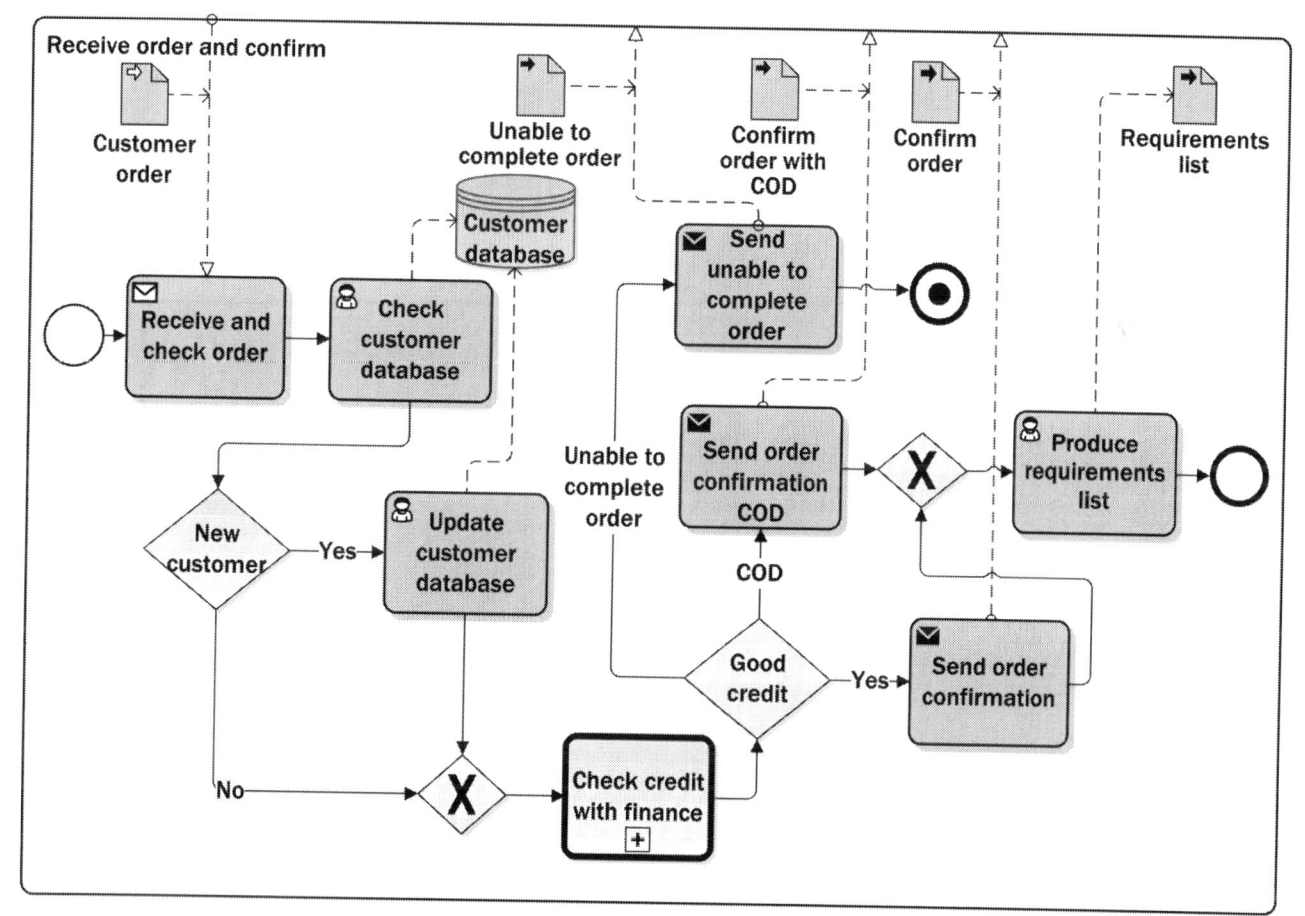

Sub-process:	**Assemble Ordered Products**

1. The customer order requirements are checked for parts availability
2. If any parts are not in stock, then a list is produced and parts ordered from the **Parts supplier**
3. The **Parts supplier** sends a delivery schedule
4. A work order is produced
5. A product delivery schedule is produced and sent to the customer
6. Parts from the **Parts supplier** are received
7. The products are assembled
8. Products are delivered to the **Warehouse**
9. The work order is completed

Admaks Publishing - BPMN Process Examples

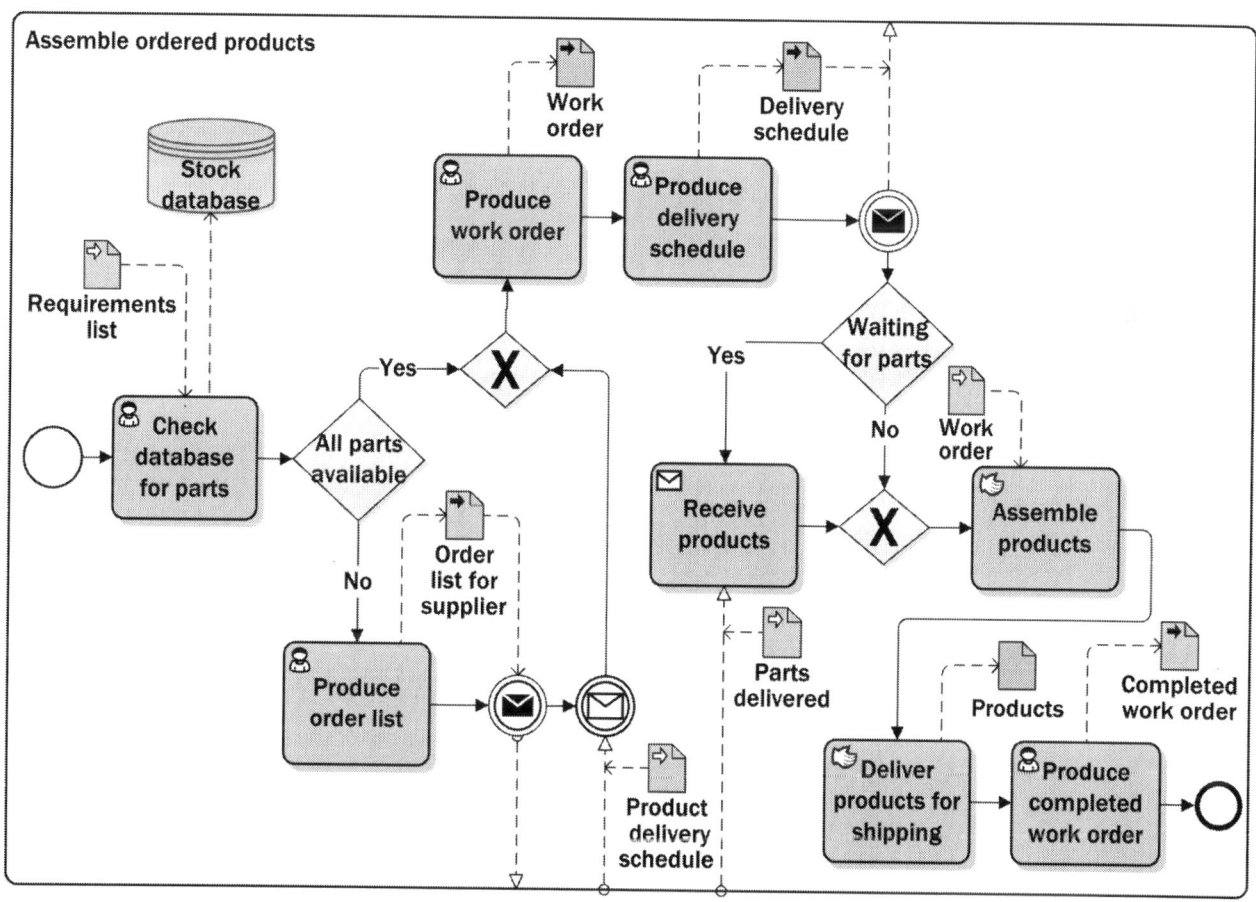

Assemble ordered products

Sub-process: Produce Invoice And Delivery Note

1. When a completed work order is received it is compared against the original order
2. An invoice for the customer is produced
3. A delivery note is produced to accompany the product
4. If the customer has a good credit rating, the invoice is sent directly to the customer
5. If the customer is COD, the invoice is forwarded to the warehouse for packing with the product
6. The delivery note is sent to the **Warehouse**

Admaks Publishing - BPMN Process Examples

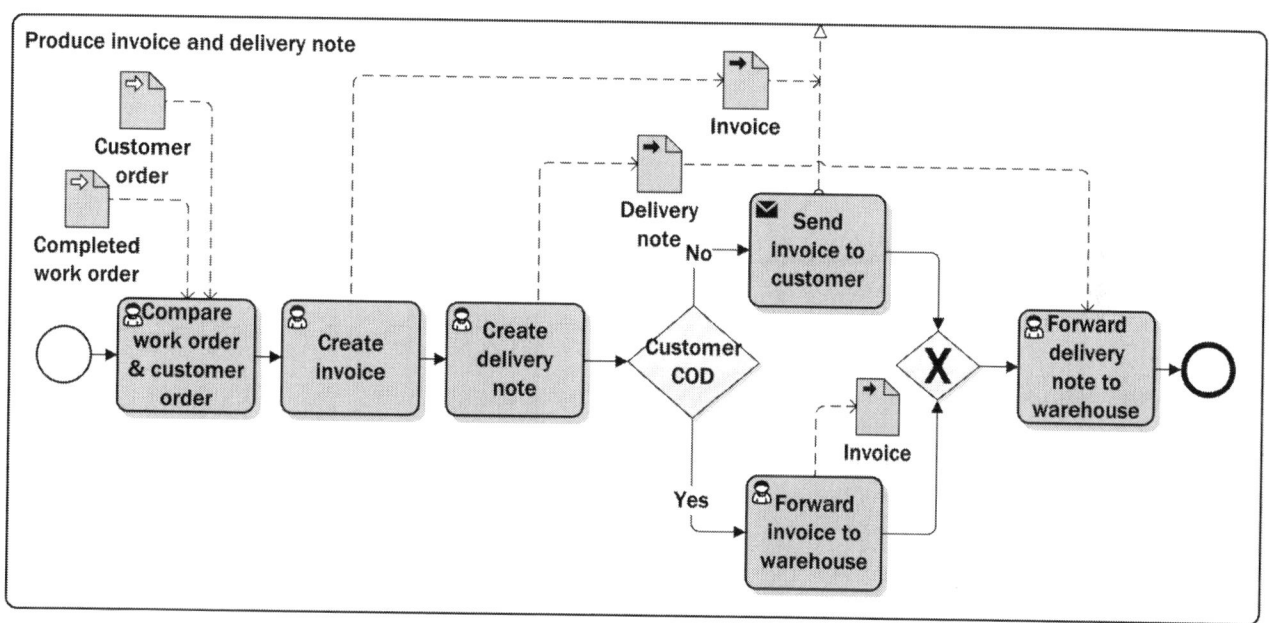

Sub-process:	**Pack And Ship Products**

1. The assembled products are received with the delivery note

2. An Invoice is received for COD customers and packed with products

3. The products are checked for special packing

4. Products are packed with or without special packing

5. The delivery note and the invoice (for COD customers) are packed with the products

6. Negotiation takes place to find the best shipping company

7. The appropriate shipping company is selected and ordered

8. A Bill of Lading is produced

9. When the shipping company arrives the goods are handed over with the Bill of Lading

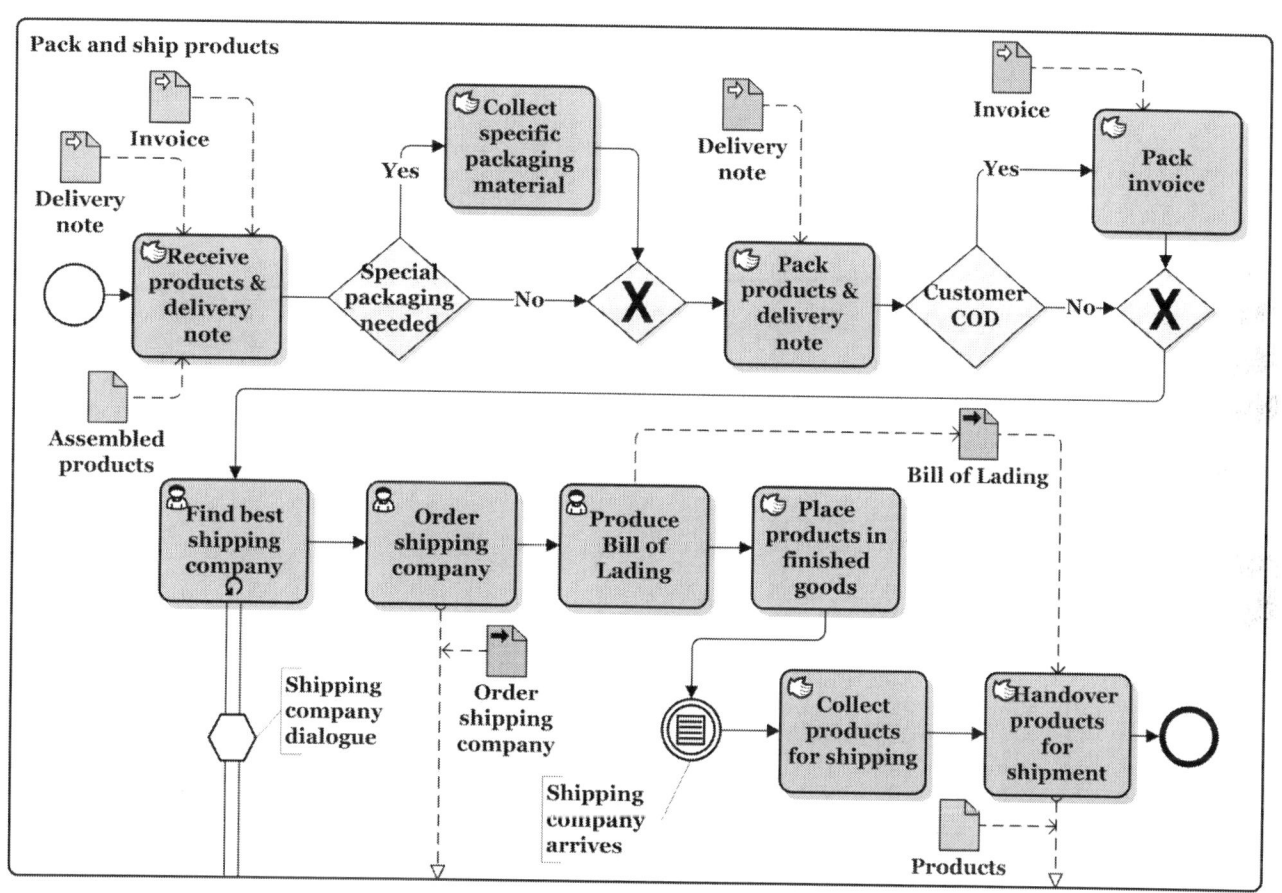

Pack and ship products

Invoice

Delivery note

Delivery note

Receive products & delivery note

Assembled products

Special packaging needed — Yes → Collect specific packaging material

No → X

Delivery note

Invoice

Pack products & delivery note

Customer COD — Yes → Pack invoice

No → X

Find best shipping company

Order shipping company

Produce Bill of Lading

Place products in finished goods

Bill of Lading

Shipping company dialogue

Order shipping company

Shipping company arrives

Collect products for shipping

Handover products for shipment

Products

Process 3 Alternative Modelling Techniques

3.1   The product artefact is shown as a data object. BPMN does not restrict the use of other artefacts, therefore a more identifiable object could describe the process more clearly.

3.2   The shipping company dialogue is shown as a conversation which is only necessary if a discussion takes place. If it is not necessary to have a discussion with the **Shipping company,** a message flow would be sufficient.

3.3   **Check credit with finance** is one of the Finance department processes and is a global call activity process call as the process is predefined by the finance department. The furniture direct process could use the process as a sub-process in the inline process. This would require the **Receive order and confirm** to be split into two separate sub-processes.

3.4   The message intermediate events used to communicate with the **Parts supplier** could be replaced by a receive and send task which would make it more descriptive.

3.5   The create invoice and delivery note could be one task, as some of the information is the same.

Process 4	Service Call Center

About the process

The service call center handles incidents which occur on a daily basis and require investigation and resolution. The process describes the steps taken when clients contact the service call center with a problem. The service call center advisor is responsible for the resolution of the incident from receipt to closure.

The service call center advisor receives a call or an email about an incident from a client. The advisor ascertains the reason for the incident and enters the explanation in the incident database. The advisor finds a contract supplier for the type of incident. A work order is raised and sent to the contract supplier. After the work has been completed the Contract supplier provides a signed completed work order.

Process collaboration

The service call center process collaborates with two separate participant processes, the Client process and the Contract supplier process.

The Service Call Center

1. A client contacts the service call center with a problem

2. The incident is logged and confirmation sent to the client

3. The service call center adviser requests a cost estimate from the contract suppliers

4. The service call center adviser raises a work order for the selected supplier

5. The contract supplier sends a completed work order

6. The service call center adviser informs the client the incident is resolved and closes the incident

7. The invoice is received from the contract suppler with a completed work order and payment is made

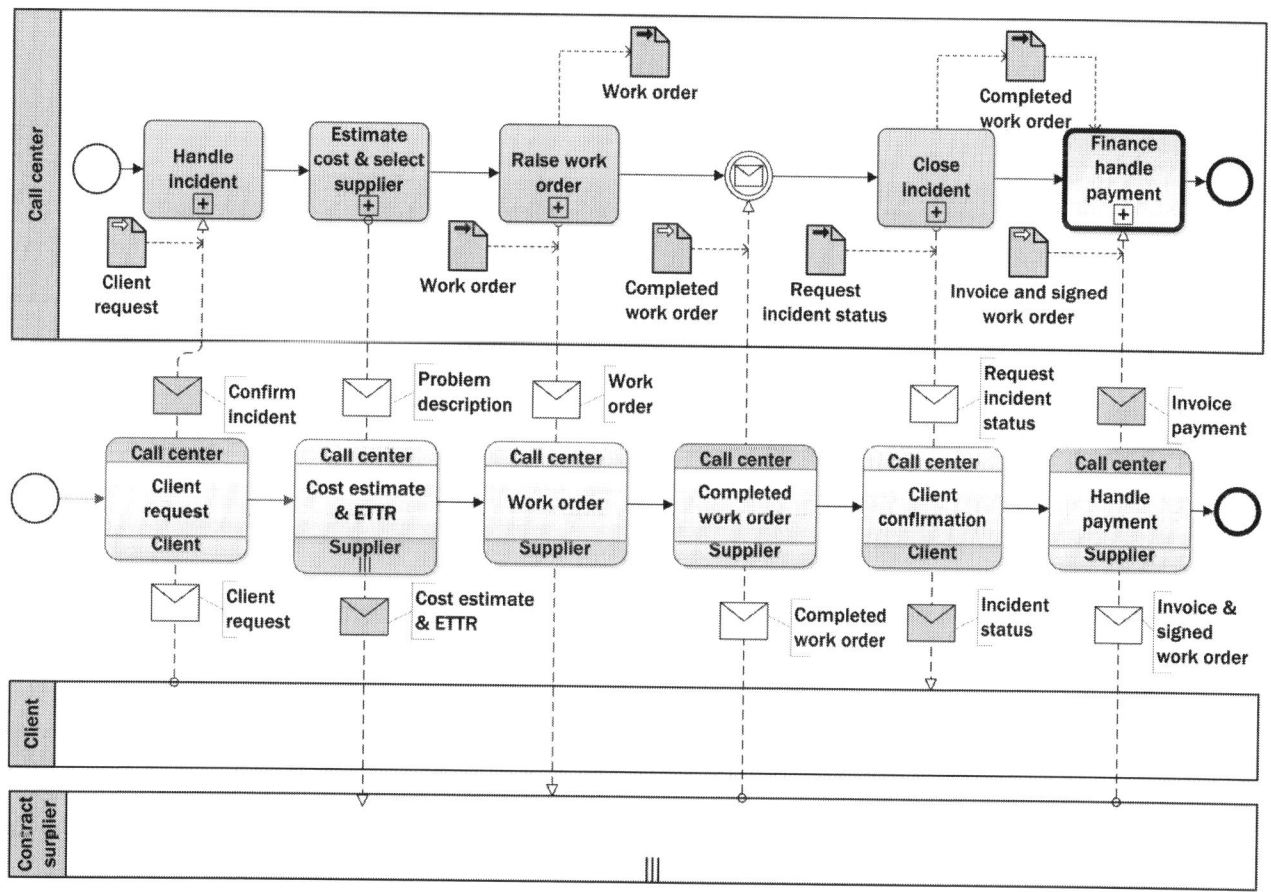

Sub-process:	Handle Incident

1. A client contacts the service call center with a problem

2. The incident is checked to ascertain whether it has already been logged

3. If it is a new incident, it is logged with a description of the problem

4. Location is identified and fault priority selected

5. Client is sent confirmation of the incident

6. Incident report is produced

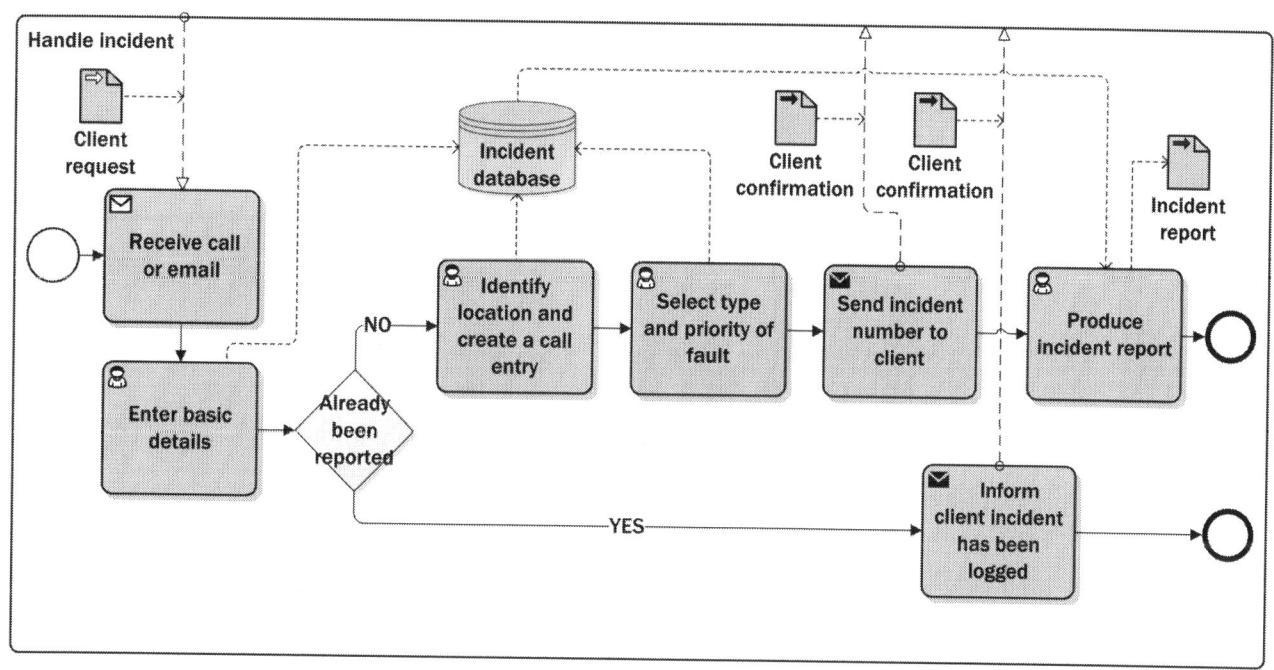

Sub-process:	Estimate Cost & Select Supplier

1. The incident is checked and cost estimated

2. If under $1000, proceed

3. If between $1000 and $5000, obtain management approval

4. Over $5000 send a request to tender

5. Send the tender to contract suppliers with problem description

6. Wait for bids until time and date has expired

7. Contract supplier is selected

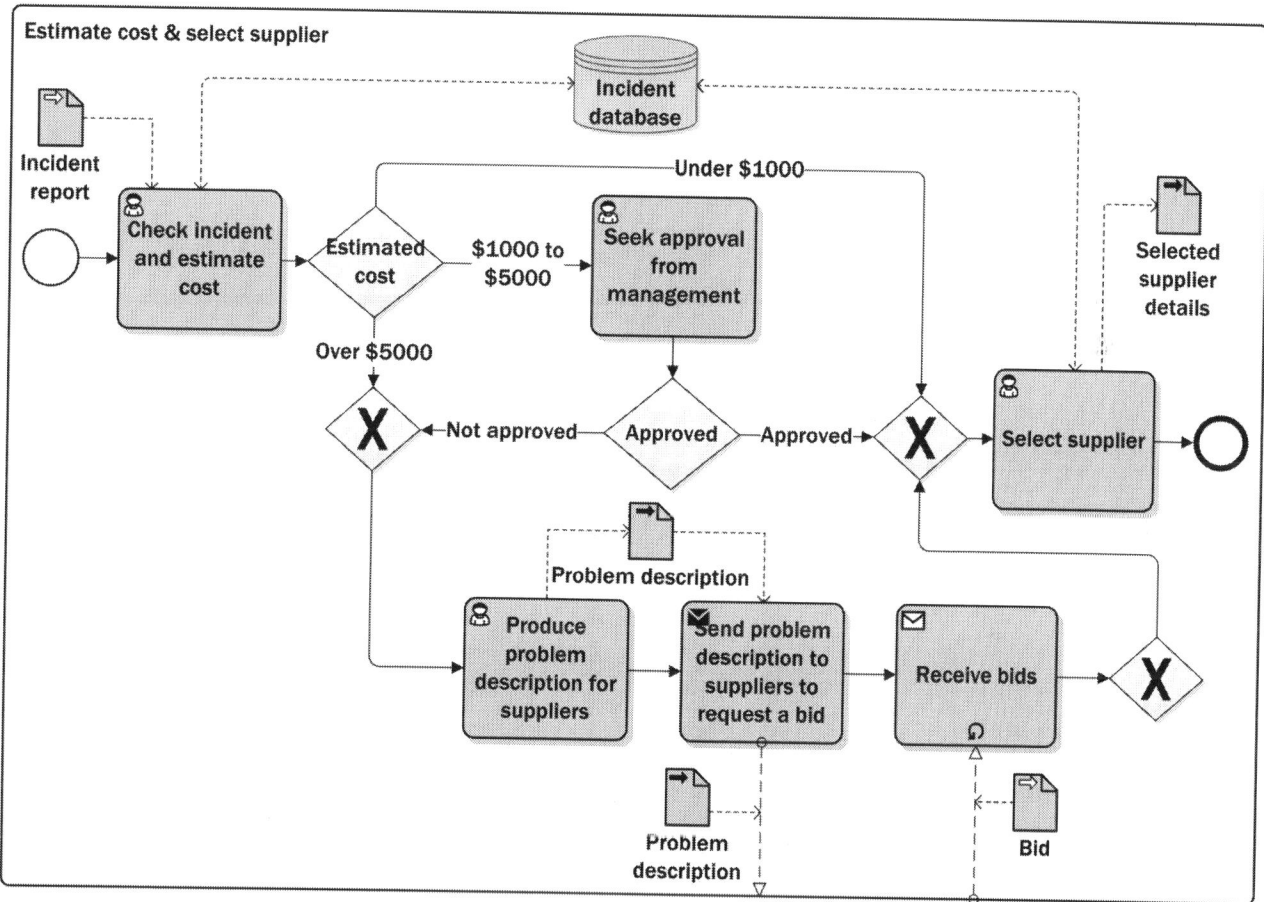

Estimate cost & select supplier

Incident report

Incident database

Check incident and estimate cost

Estimated cost

$1000 to $5000

Seek approval from management

Under $1000

Selected supplier details

Over $5000

Not approved

Approved

Approved

Select supplier

Produce problem description for suppliers

Problem description

Send problem description to suppliers to request a bid

Receive bids

Problem description

Bid

Sub-process:	**Process Work Order**

1. A work order is raised and the supplier details are entered

2. An ETTR is requested from the supplier

3. An ETTR is received

4. A work order is produced

5. The work order is sent to the supplier

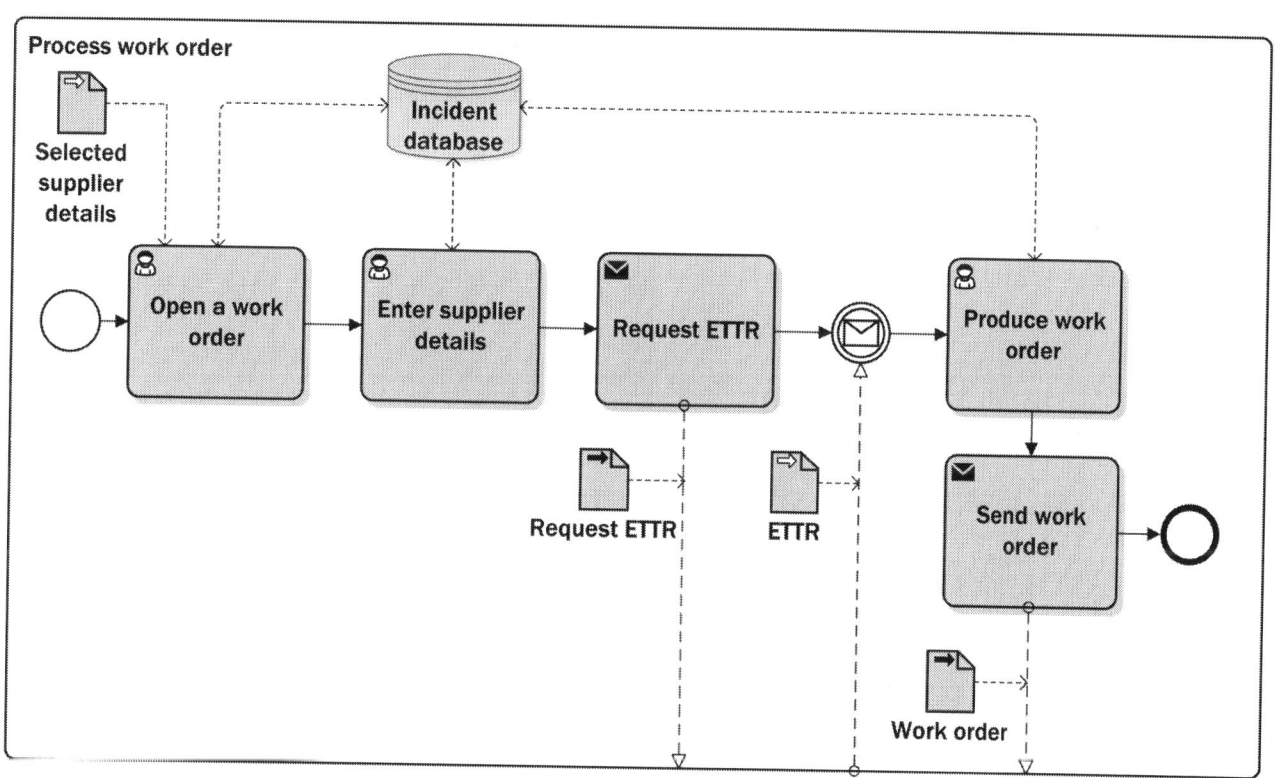

Sub-process:	**Close Incident**

1. The completed work order is received and checked

2. An incident status is requested from the client

3. The client confirmation is received

4. If the status response is positive, the incident is closed

5. If the status response is negative, a status request is sent to the contract supplier

6. A status response is received from the contract supplier

7. The process waits until a positive status response received

8. The incident is closed

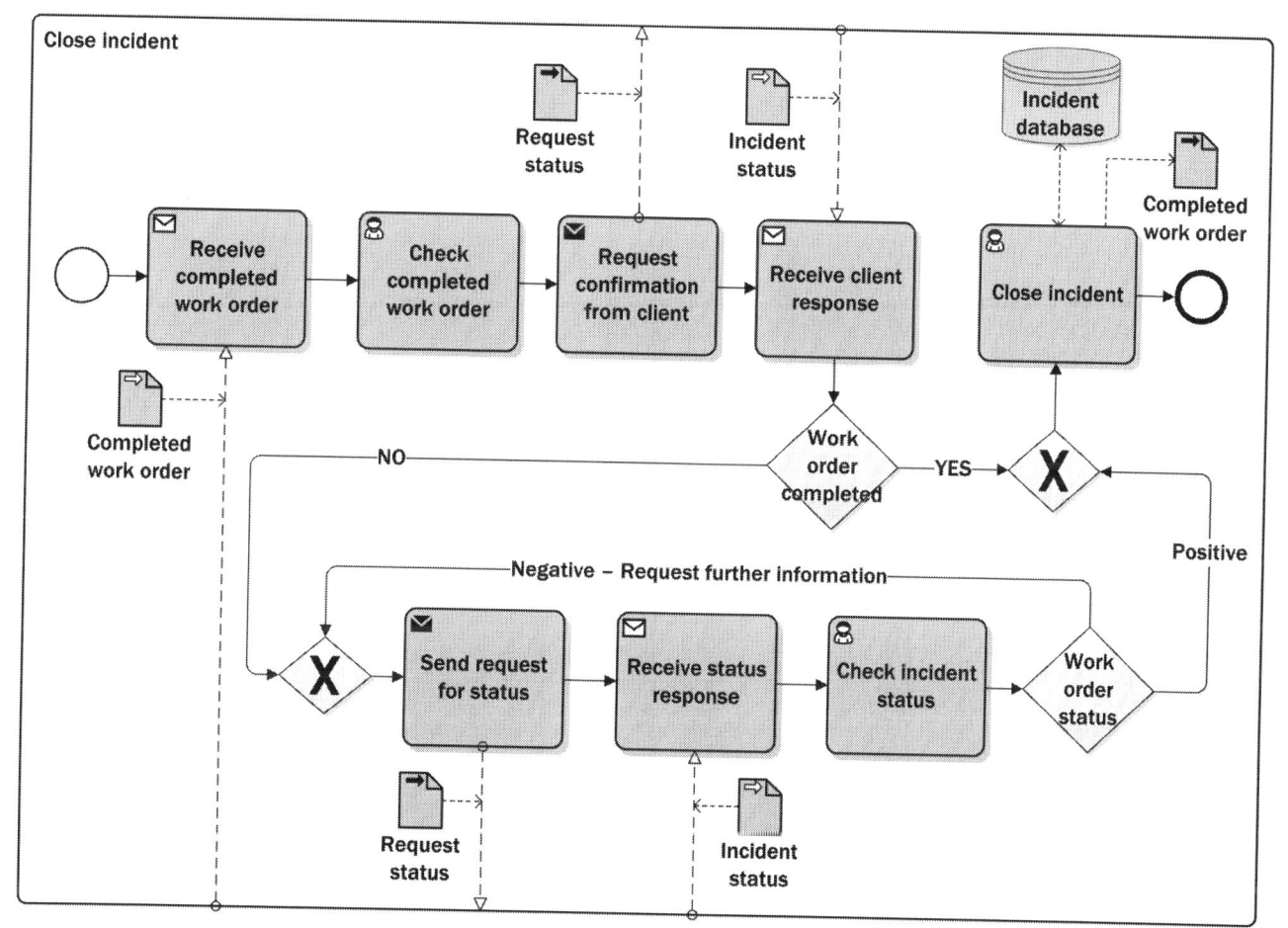

Process 4 Alternative Modelling Techniques

4.1   **Request bids and receive bids** could be depicted with send and receive tasks instead of message intermediate events.

4.2   The choreography task **Work order** has an initiating message and no return message. A return message would be useful at this stage of the process work flow status.

4.3   The choreography sequence shows a message flow triggering a message intermediate event. As the completed work order is handled by the **Close incident** sub-process, an alternative could be to connect to the boundary of the sub-process.

4.4   The **Receive bids** task, could be depicted with a timer intermediate boundary event with a sequence flow used for overdue bids. This will inform the contract supplier the bid was not received in the time/date allocated.

4.5   If a request incident status from the supplier is positive and client status is negative, it would be necessary to loop between the client and the supplier until receiving a positive response from both, before closing the incident.

Process 5   Company Procurement

About the process

The company procurement process begins when an order is placed by an employee for a product or service and ends when the product or service is ordered.

There can be many suppliers, however the interface to the suppliers is always the same. If a supplier selection is required, a selection procedure takes place before ordering.

Process collaboration

The Company Procurement process requires collaboration between two separate participants; the company department requiring a product or service and the supplier process used to order products or services. The pool of the collaborating suppliers is depicted by a multi instance pool symbol.

Overview:	Company Procurement

1. An employee requests a product or service and supplies the relevant documents

2. The product or service is assessed by procurement to decide whether a tender is required

3. If a tender is required, an Invitation to Tender (ITT) is sent to selected suppliers

4. A minimum number of ITT's are sent, depending on the business rules of product or service cost

5. If bids are required they can be received at anytime up to the time/date of the bid closure

6. All bids are checked and a supplier is selected, based on the company business rules

7. Procurement sends an order for the product or service to the selected supplier

8. The product or service order details are sent to the employee

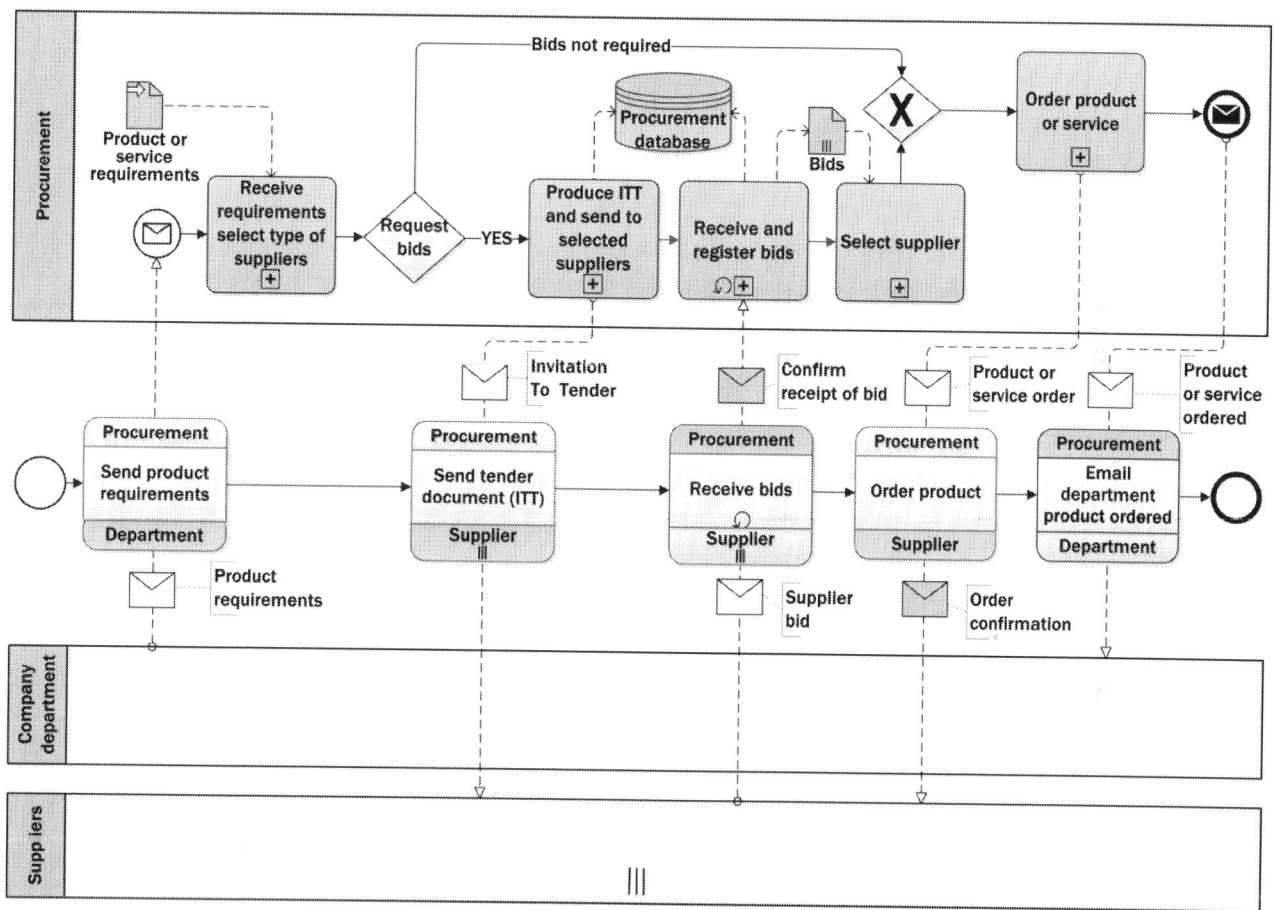

Sub-process:	**Receive Requirements Select Type Of Suppliers**

1. Product or service requirements are received

2. The product or service is assessed

3. If only one supplier is available, a justification is produced and details documented

4. If there are framework contracts available, they are selected and a list of preferred suppliers is produced

5. If the product or service cost is under $500, a supplier is selected and the details are documented

Admaks Publishing - BPMN Process Examples

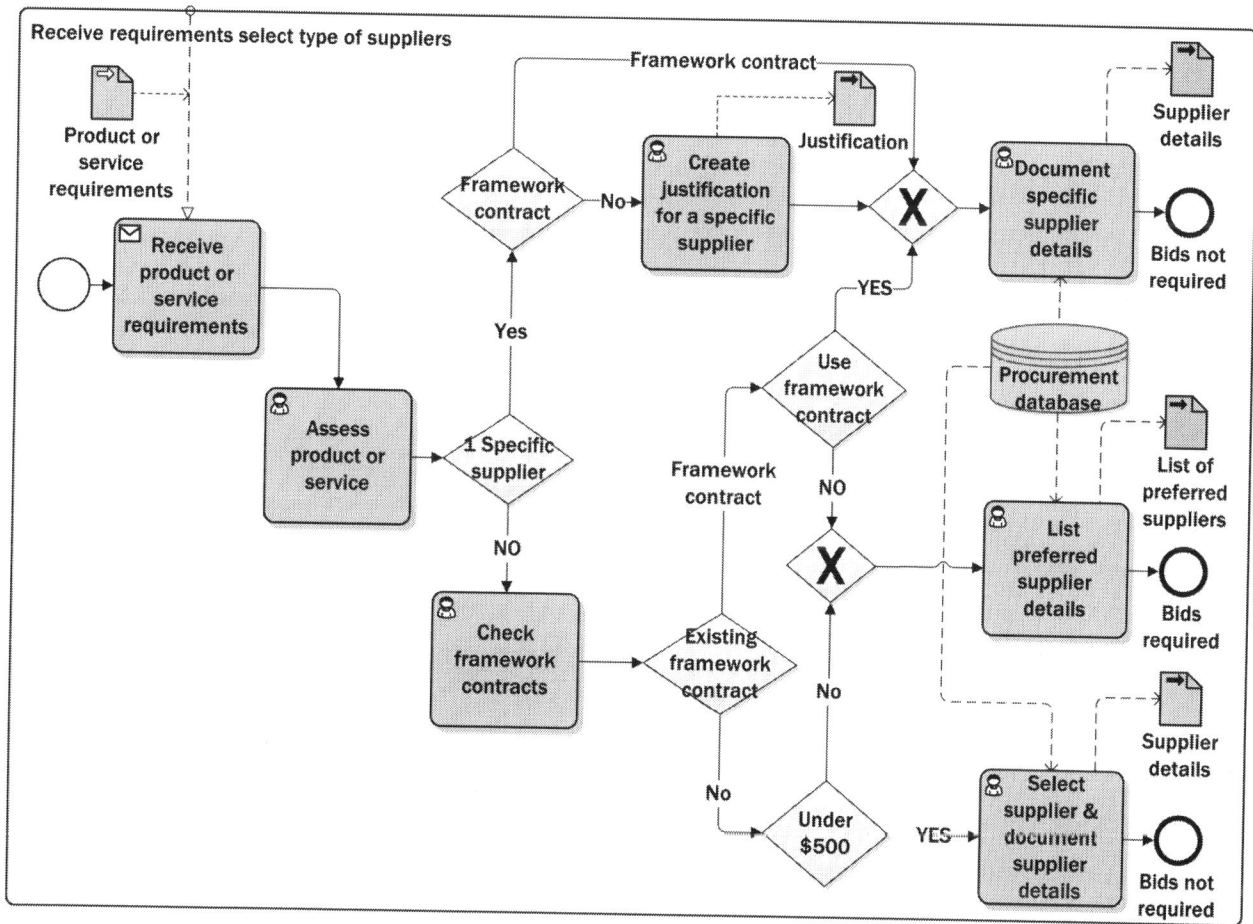

1. The requirements are checked and the cost of products or services estimated

2. The cost determines the type of procedure

3. Under $5000 only one supplier is required

4. Between $5000 and $25000 a minimum of three suppliers are required

5. Over $25000 a minimum of five suppliers are required

6. An Invitation To Tender is produced

7. The ITT is sent to selected suppliers

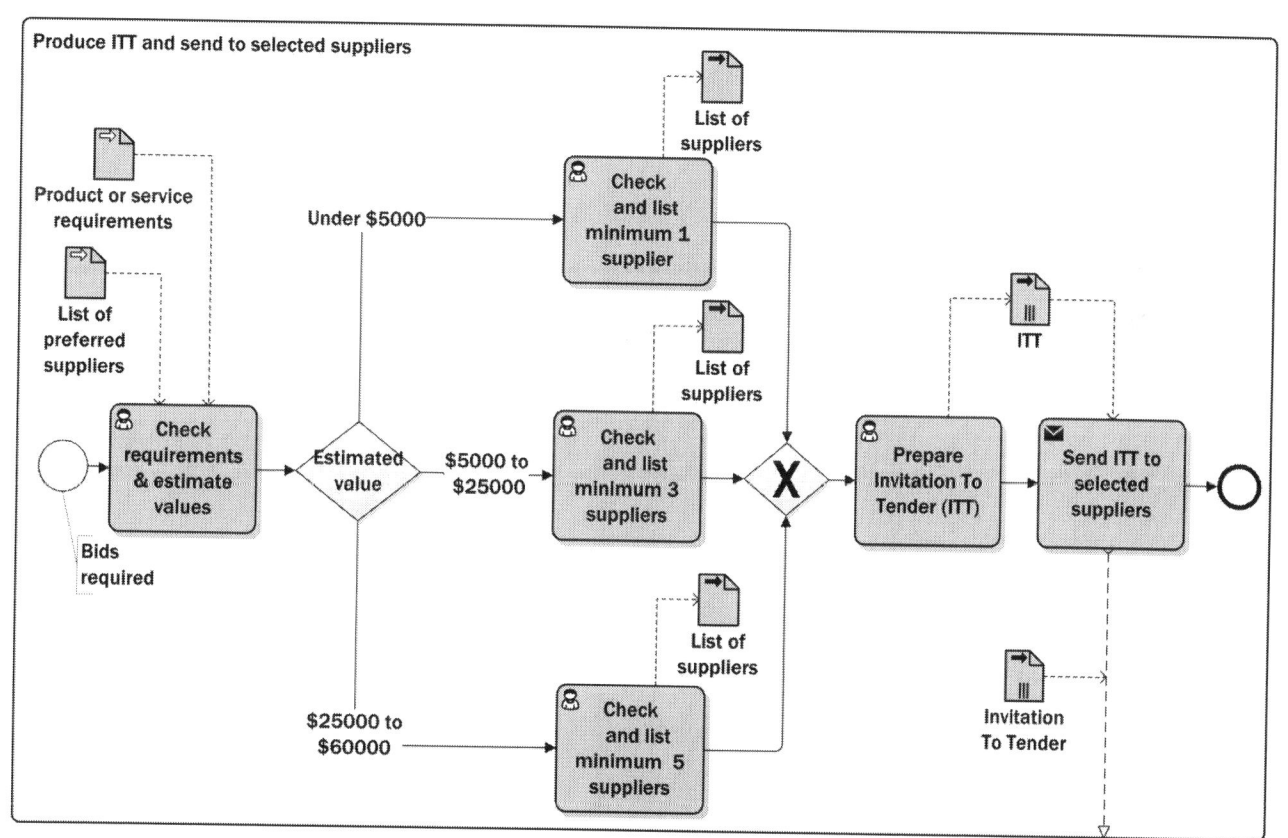

Produce ITT and send to selected suppliers

Product or service requirements

List of preferred suppliers

Check requirements & estimate values

Bids required

Estimated value

Under $5000

$5000 to $25000

$25000 to $60000

List of suppliers

Check and list minimum 1 supplier

Check and list minimum 3 suppliers

Check and list minimum 5 suppliers

List of suppliers

List of suppliers

ITT

Prepare Invitation To Tender (ITT)

Send ITT to selected suppliers

Invitation To Tender

Sub-process: Receive And Register Bids

1. Bids are received up to the bid closure time/date

2. The business rules bidding procedures determine whether bids are opened or not

3. If bids are not to be opened until bid closure, they are stored unopened

4. If bids may be opened, they are opened, checked and stored

5. Suppliers are sent confirmation on bids received

6. If bids are received after closure date, the supplier is sent a **Time & date elapsed on bids**, response

7. Bids are collated and reviewed under a predetermined business rule criteria

8. A supplier is selected and the supplier's details are documented

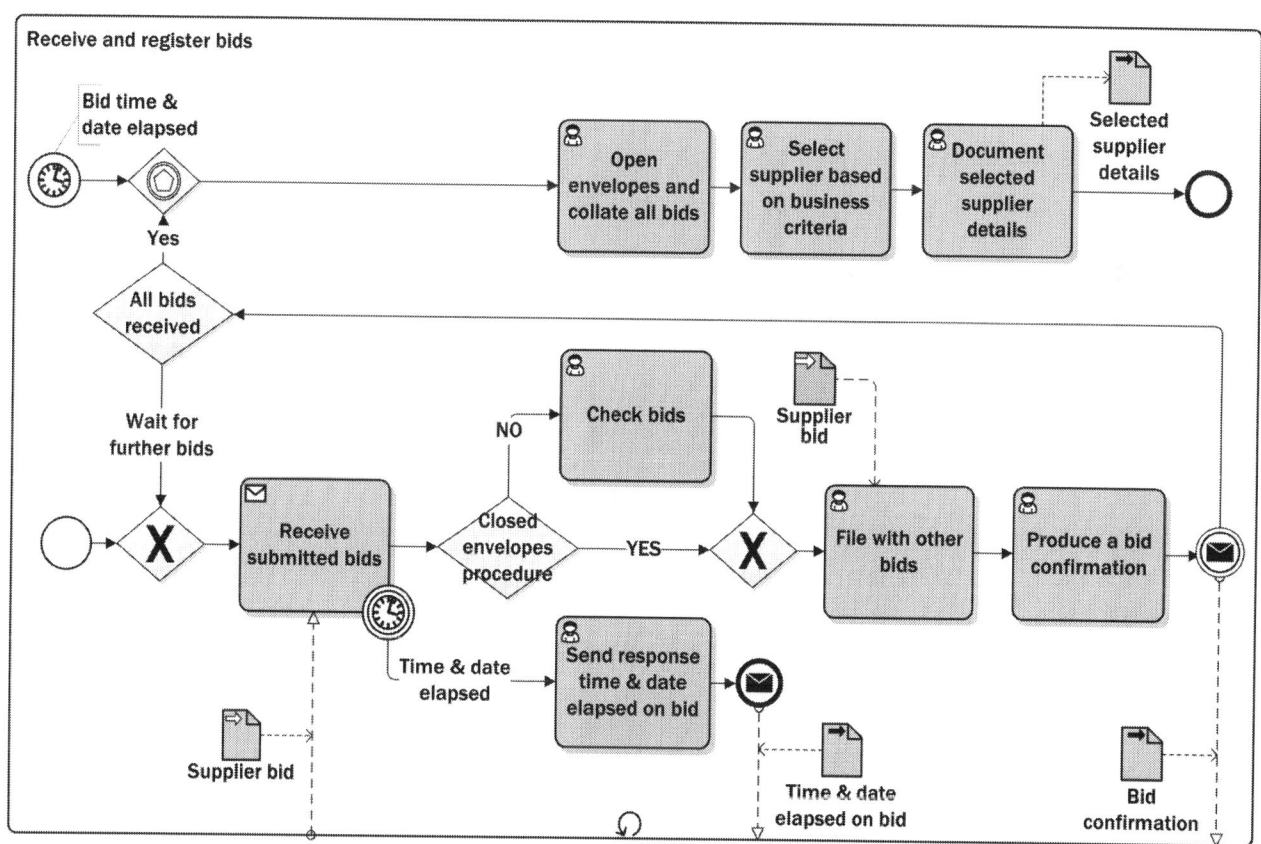

Receive and register bids

Bid time & date elapsed

Yes

All bids received

Wait for further bids

Open envelopes and collate all bids

Select supplier based on business criteria

Document selected supplier details

Selected supplier details

Check bids

Supplier bid

NO

Receive submitted bids

Closed envelopes procedure

YES

File with other bids

Produce a bid confirmation

Time & date elapsed

Send response time & date elapsed on bid

Supplier bid

Time & date elapsed on bid

Bid confirmation

Sub-process:	**Order Product Or Service**

1. The supplier details and bid are checked and confirmed

2. The order information is sent to finance, to check departmental budget availability

3. Finance confirms if product or service can be ordered

4. If a budget cannot be assigned, the employee is sent **Unable to order**

5. If a budget is assigned, an order is produced and sent to the supplier

6. When product or service is ordered, the employee is sent **Product or service ordered**

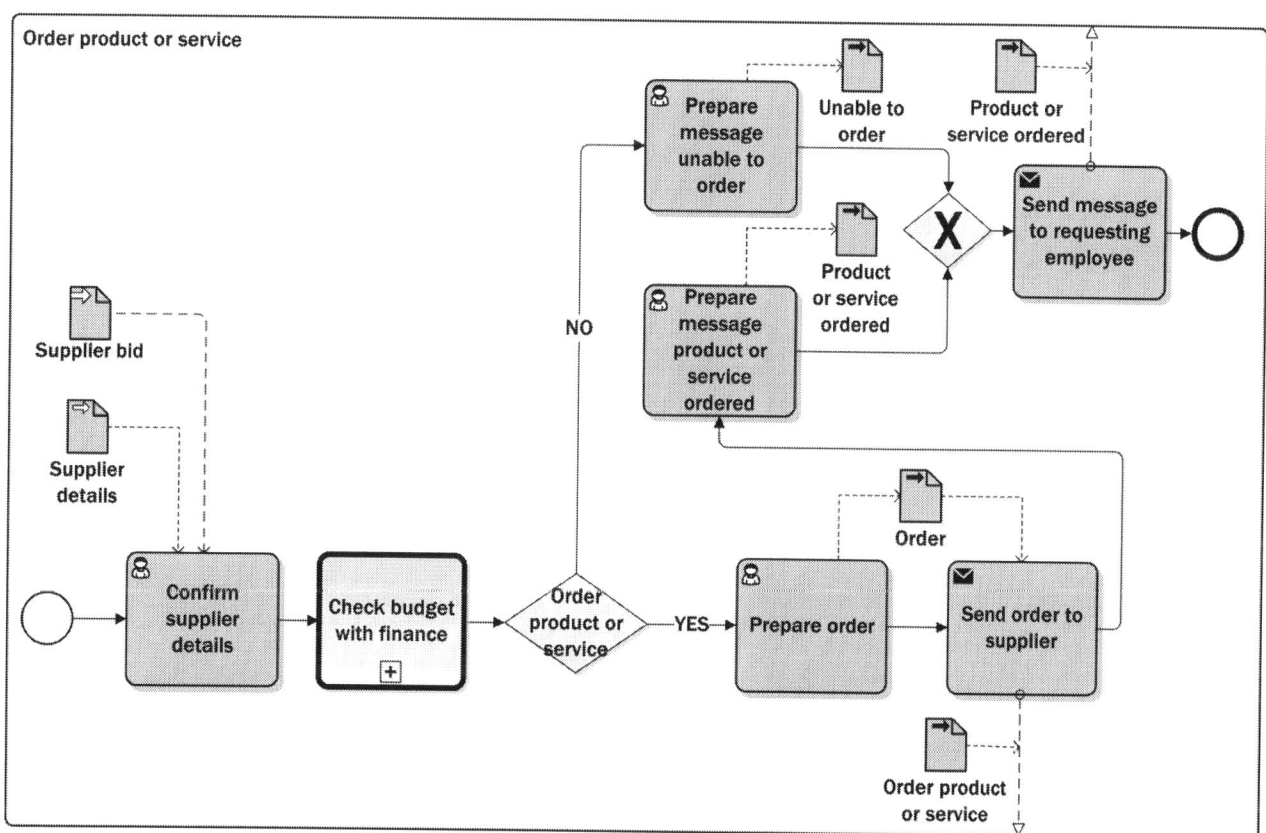

5.1   The inline process is started on receipt of a message depicted by a message start event. A none start event could be used instead, with the message flow connected to the **Receive requirements select type of supplier,** sub-process.

5.2   The inline process ends and sends a message **Product or service ordered,** depicted by a message end event. A none end event could be used instead, with the message flow connected from the **Order product or service,** sub-process.

5.2   As an ITT is sent to the supplier, a response from the supplier that the ITT was received could be depicted.

5.3   The justification for a specific supplier without a frame contract would need management approval which could be included in the BPD.

5.4   The **Check budget with finance,** sub-process would be more useful as part of **Produce ITT and send to selected suppliers**, sub-process. This would control whether to send an ITT or an order if the budget was not available.

5.5   The **Receive and register bids**, is a looping sub-process. An annotation with an expression describing the number of instances could be added.

Process 6   Worldwide Annual Reporting

About the process

An international organisation requires annual reports from all regions and countries worldwide. The reports are entered by local staff and checked by the regional office before being forwarded to HQ. High priority annual reports are entered by local personnel in each country or by regional staff and checked by HQ. The reporting database is available to all countries, regions and HQ. Reports are categorised and prioritised.

HQ is accountable for all reporting and publishing. Regional offices are responsible for their own reports and verification of reports from countries in their region. Country offices are responsible for their own annual reports.

Process collaboration

The World Wide Reporting process requires collaboration between three separate participant processes; HQ process, Regional Office process and Country Office process.

Overview:	**Worldwide Annual Reporting Overview**

1. Company HQ starts the reporting process by sending an initiating report document to each region

2. HQ proceeds to draft HQ reports

3. Each region starts the regional process on receipt of the HQ initiating report document and sends out an initiating report document to each of their country offices

4. Each country within a specific region starts the country process on receipt of the regional initiating report document

5. Completed priority reports are reviewed by the regions and sent to HQ for review before publishing

6. Completed non-priority reports are reviewed by the regional offices and sent to HQ for publishing

7. Regional offices check country reports and negotiate changes with the country if necessary

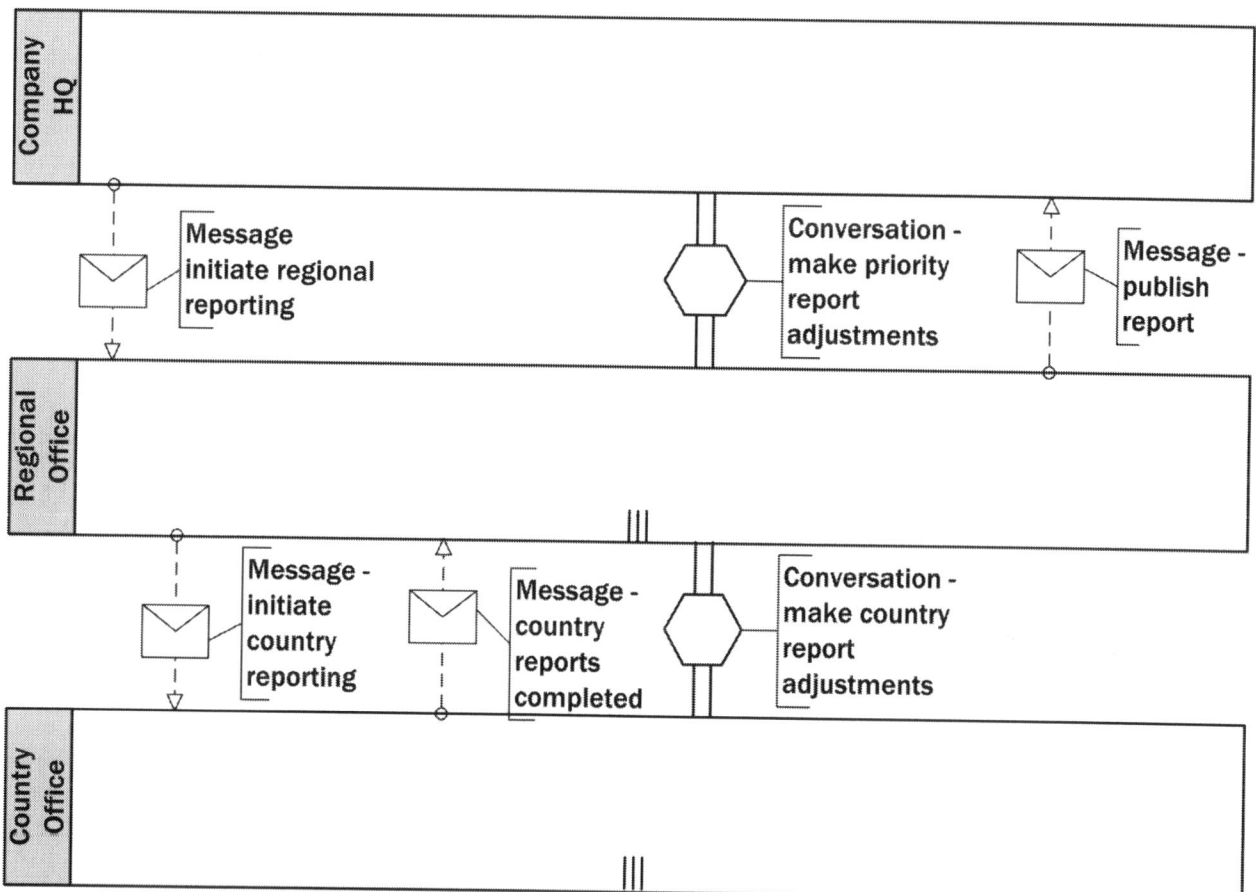

6.1 Worldwide Annual Reporting Headquarters (HQ Process)

About the process

HQ initiates the process for each regional office by sending a list of report requirements.

HQ drafts reports that only concern HQ. HQ receives priority reports from the regional offices, makes changes and adjustments if necessary. Completed reports are received from the regional offices and published.

Process collaboration

HQ collaborates with each regional office process.

1. The reporting is initiated by HQ which sends the report requirements list to each region

2. HQ drafts HQ reports

3. HQ checks priority reports received from the regions and makes changes and adjustments if necessary

4. When priority reports have satisfied both HQ and the regional office, the reports are sent for publishing

5. Regional offices send completed non-priority reports to HQ for publishing

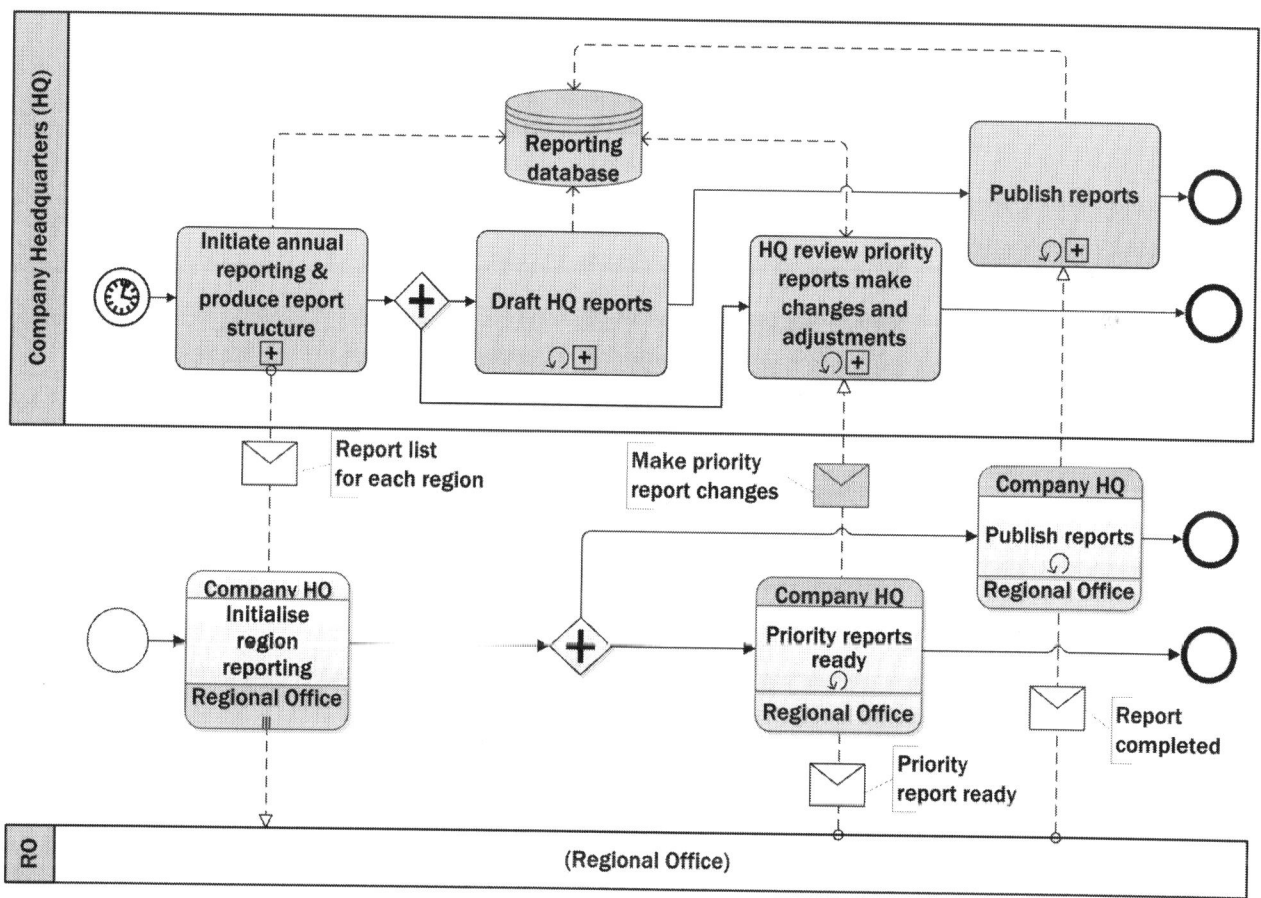

Sub-process:	**Initiate Annual Reporting & Produce Report Structures**

1. Log-in to the reporting database

2. The annual report project leader downloads a list of required reports and prioritises, inserting deadlines if necessary

3. Report formats are produced

4. Reviewers selected

5. Regional report lists are produced and sent to each region

6. HQ report list is generated and the report coordinator informed

7. Log-out of database

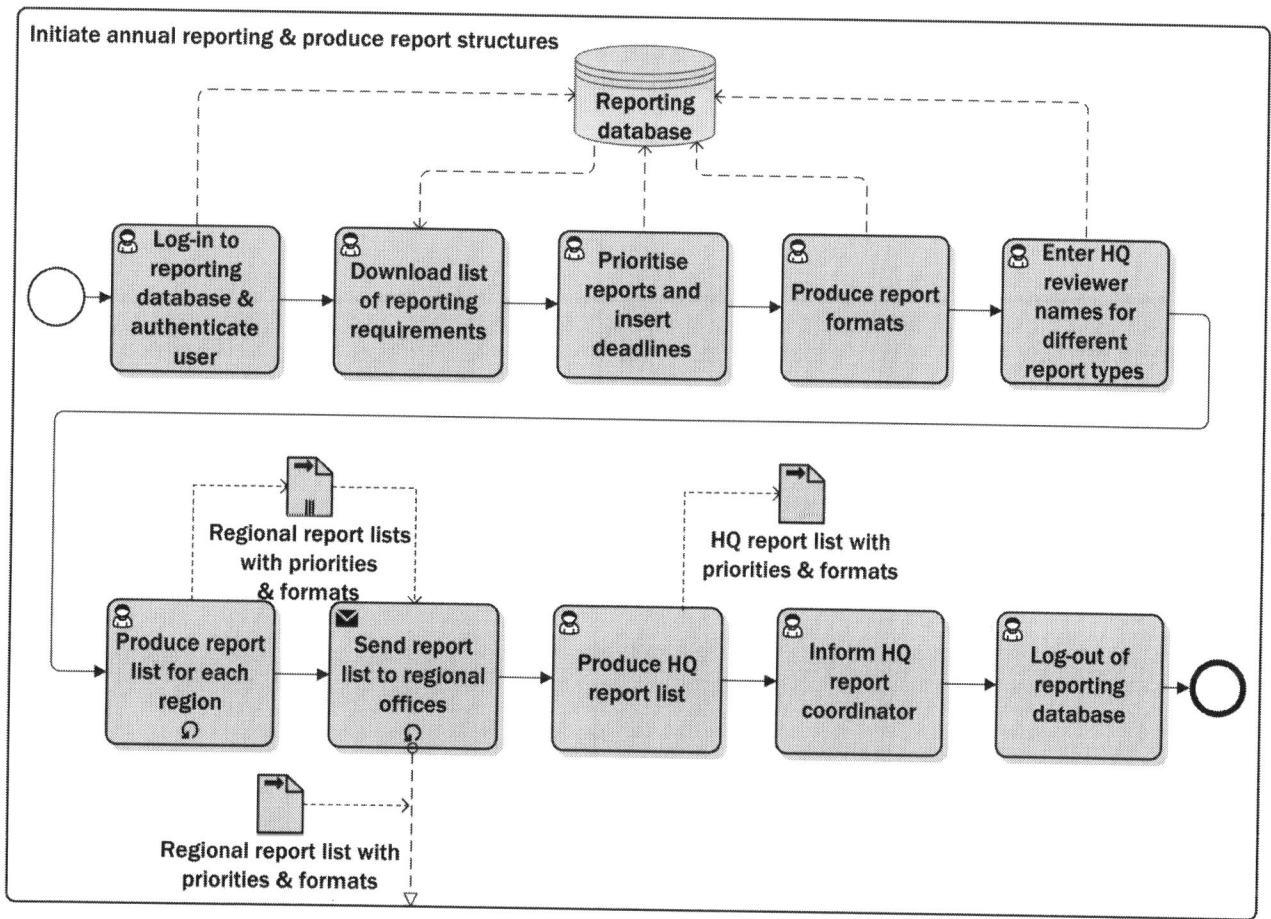

Initiate annual reporting & produce report structures

Reporting database

Log-in to reporting database & authenticate user

Download list of reporting requirements

Prioritise reports and insert deadlines

Produce report formats

Enter HQ reviewer names for different report types

Regional report lists with priorities & formats

HQ report list with priorities & formats

Produce report list for each region

Send report list to regional offices

Produce HQ report list

Inform HQ report coordinator

Log-out of reporting database

Regional report list with priorities & formats

Sub-process:	Draft HQ Reports

1. Log-in to the reporting database

2. Download the HQ report status

3. Draft reports

4. Set reporting status

5. Log-out of reporting database

6. The sub-process loops until all HQ reports are drafted and checked

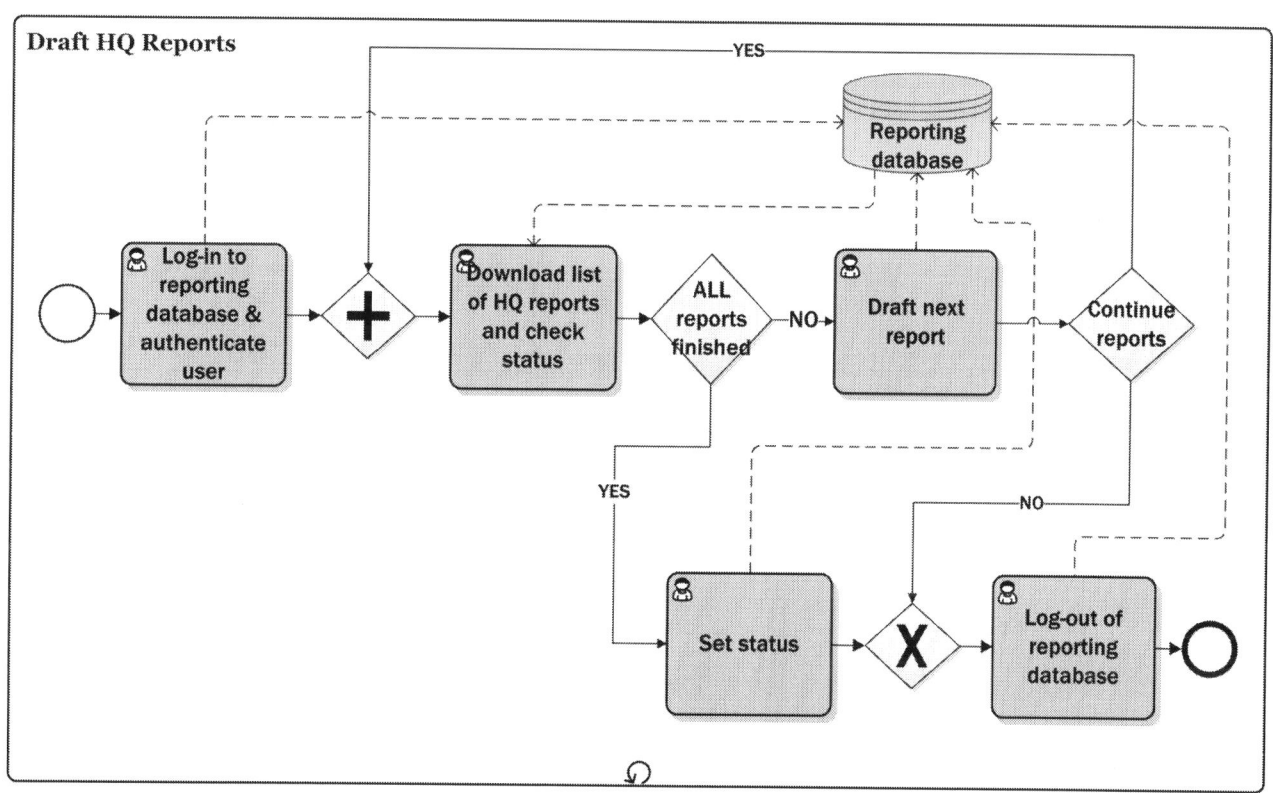

Draft HQ Reports

Sub-process: HQ Review Priority Reports Make Changes And Adjustments

1. The sub-process is initiated when a region sends a priority report ready for review

2. Log-in to the reporting database

3. Priority reports are reviewed and changed if required

4. Report status is set

5. A list of changes are sent to the specific region

6. Log-out of reporting database

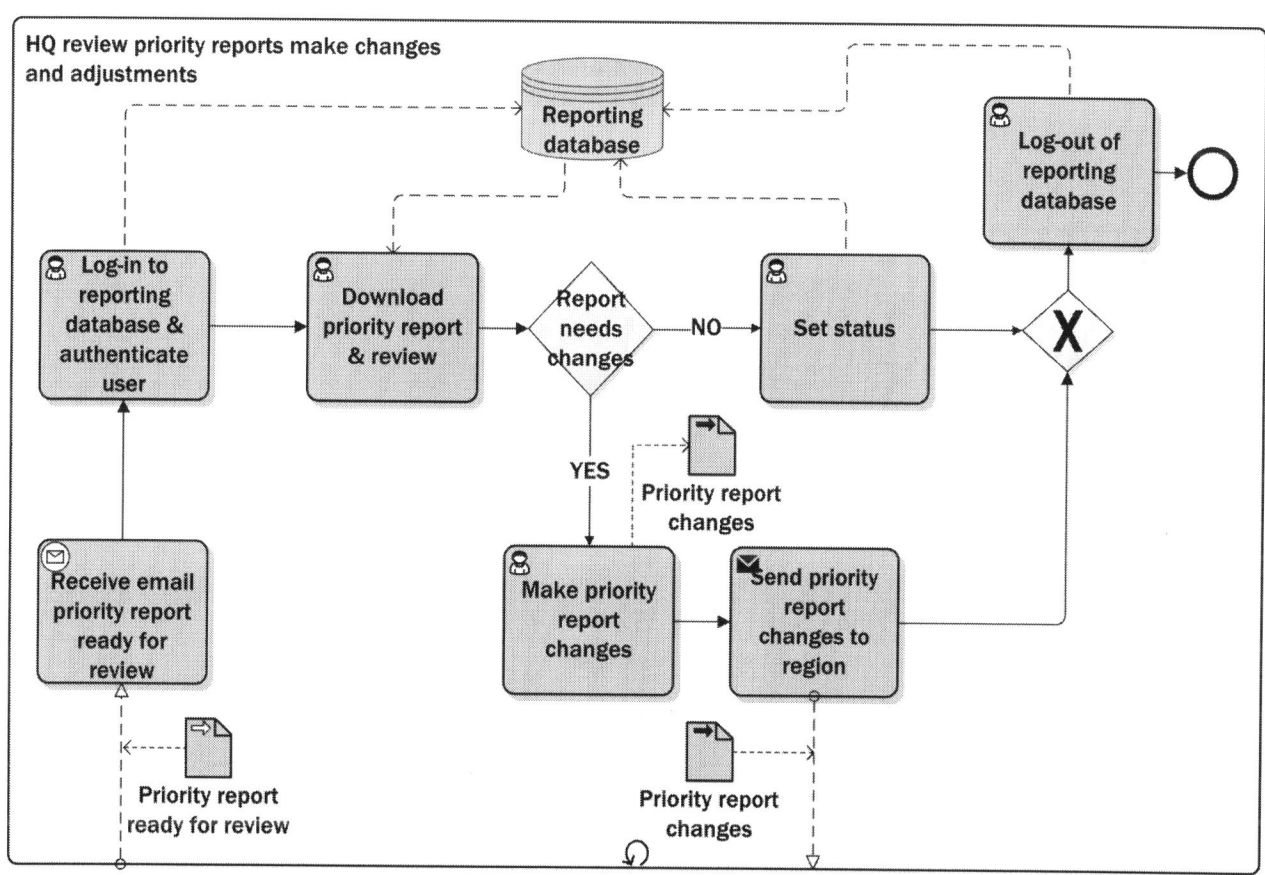

HQ review priority reports make changes and adjustments

Reporting database

Log-in to reporting database & authenticate user

Download priority report & review

Report needs changes

NO

Set status

Log-out of reporting database

YES

Priority report changes

Receive email priority report ready for review

Make priority report changes

Send priority report changes to region

Priority report ready for review

Priority report changes

Sub-process:	Publish Reports

1. Emails are received informing HQ that a regional report is ready for publishing
2. When HQ reports are completed all reports are published
3. Log-in to the reporting database
4. Each report is archived and converted to web base format
5. The status is set to report published
6. Log-out of reporting database

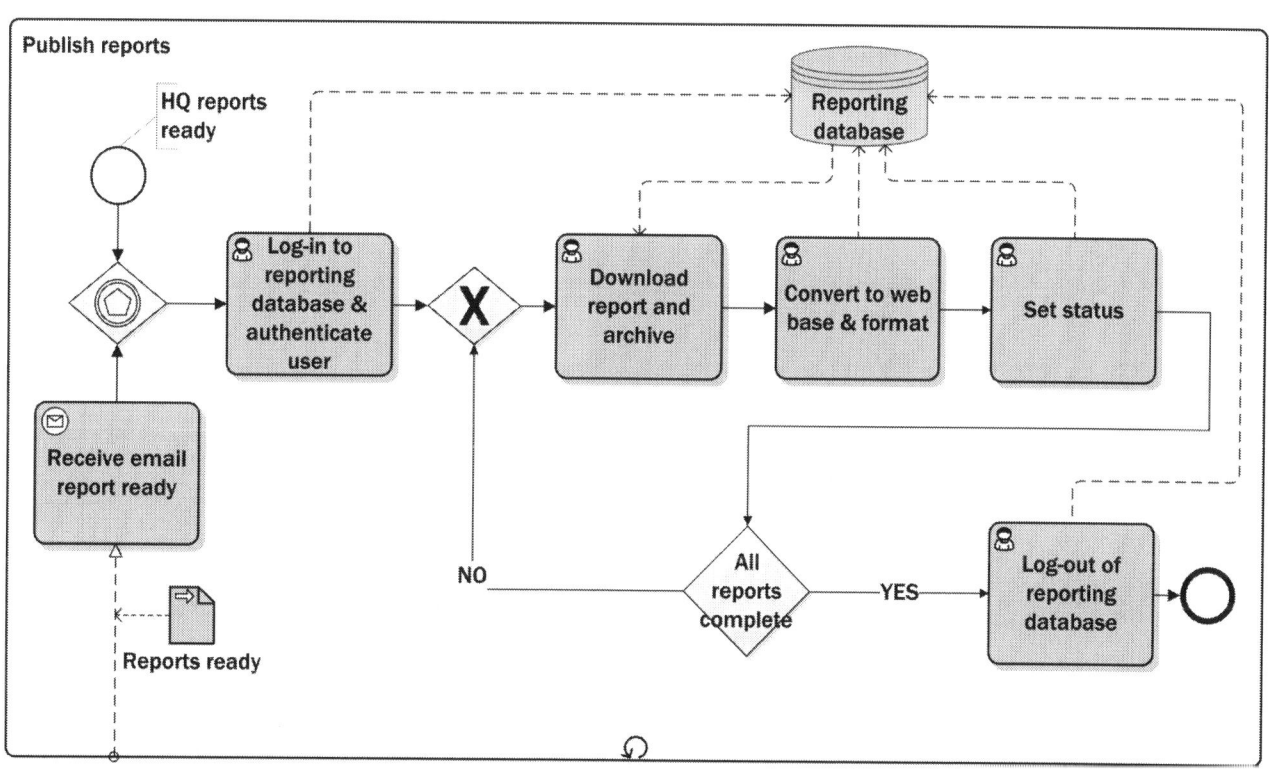

Publish reports

HQ reports ready

Log-in to reporting database & authenticate user

Reporting database

Download report and archive

Convert to web base & format

Set status

Receive email report ready

Reports ready

All reports complete

NO

YES

Log-out of reporting database

6.2 Worldwide Annual Reporting Regional Offices (RO Process)

About the process

The regional office reporting process is initiated by HQ. HQ sends the list of reports required from the region and the countries within their region.

The regional offices receive country reports and check for any adjustments. If adjustments are required, the report is returned with the suggested changes.

The regional offices document priority reports and send them to HQ for review. HQ and the regional offices adjust the priority reports.

Process Collaboration

The regional offices collaborate with both HQ and with each of their country offices.

1. The reporting is initiated by HQ, which sends the list of reports required to the regional offices

2. Regional offices allocate reporters and produce a country report list

3. Country offices are sent the list of reports required

4. Regions draft their own reports

5. Countries complete reports and inform their regional office

6. Regions review the changes in priority reports from HQ and make adjustments

7. Regions review country reports, make changes and adjustments

8. Regions inform HQ when reports are ready for publishing

Admaks Publishing - BPMN Process Examples

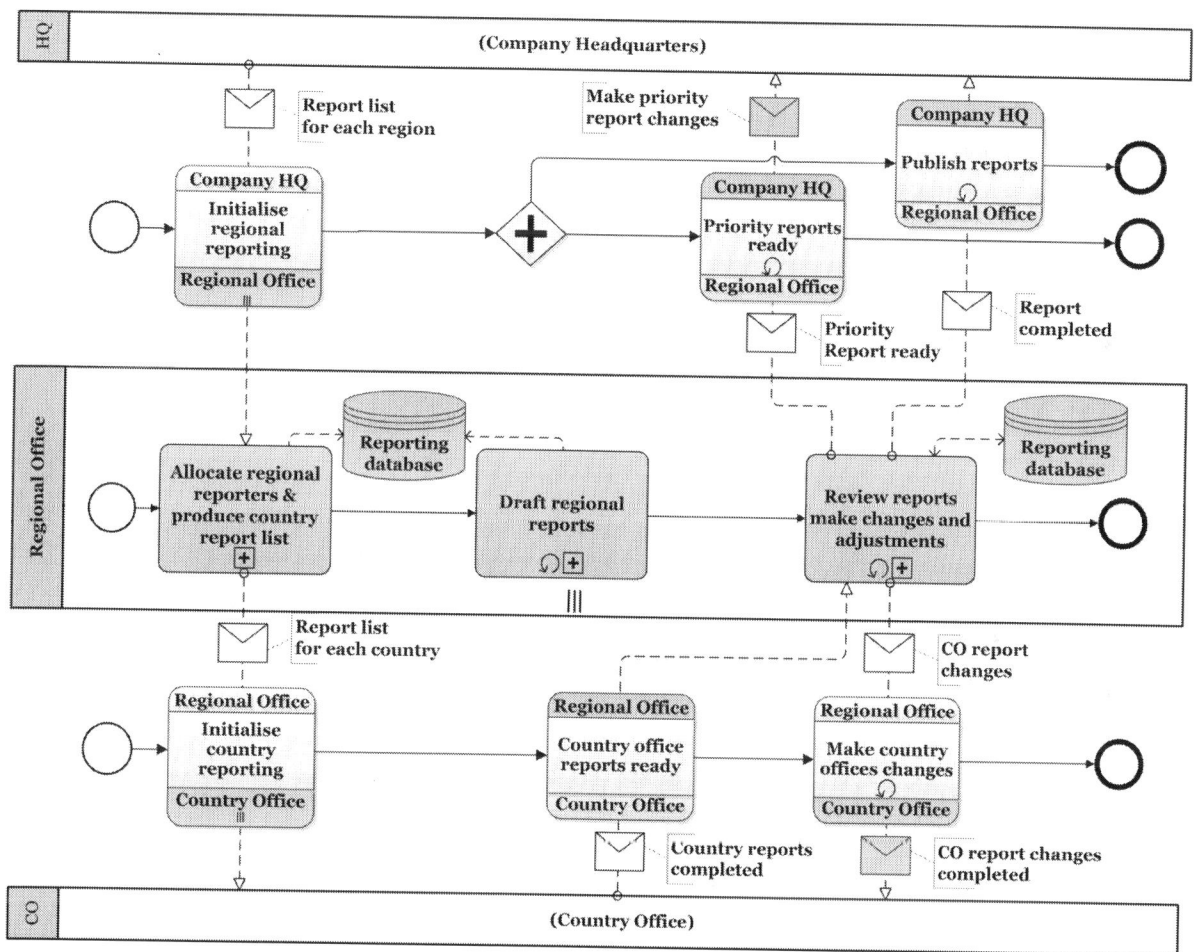

Sub-process: Allocate Regional Reporters & Produce Country Reporting List

1. Receive list of regional reports

2. Log-in to the reporting database

3. Regional report list is downloaded

4. Regional reporters are allocated

5. A list of specific regional reports is produced

6. A list of reports is produced for each country in their region

7. Country office reporting is initiated

8. The list of required country reports is sent to each country office

9. Log-out of reporting database

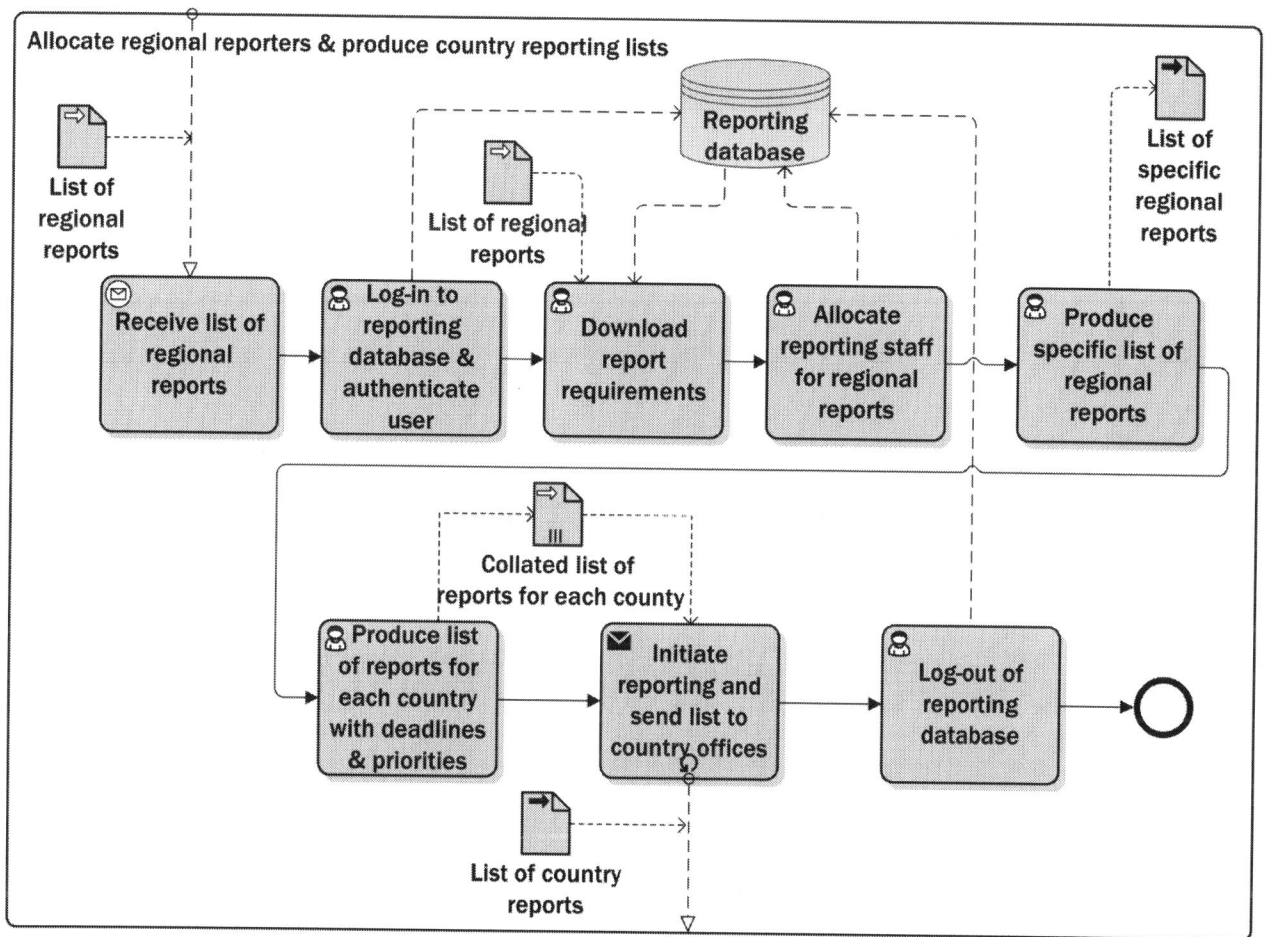

Allocate regional reporters & produce country reporting lists

List of regional reports

List of regional reports

Reporting database

List of specific regional reports

Receive list of regional reports

Log-in to reporting database & authenticate user

Download report requirements

Allocate reporting staff for regional reports

Produce specific list of regional reports

Collated list of reports for each county

Produce list of reports for each country with deadlines & priorities

Initiate reporting and send list to country offices

Log-out of reporting database

List of country reports

Sub-process:	Draft Regional Reports

1. Log-in to the reporting database
2. The report list is checked for regional reports
3. The next report is drafted
4. Check for further reports
5. Log-out of reporting database
6. Sub-process loops until all reports are drafted

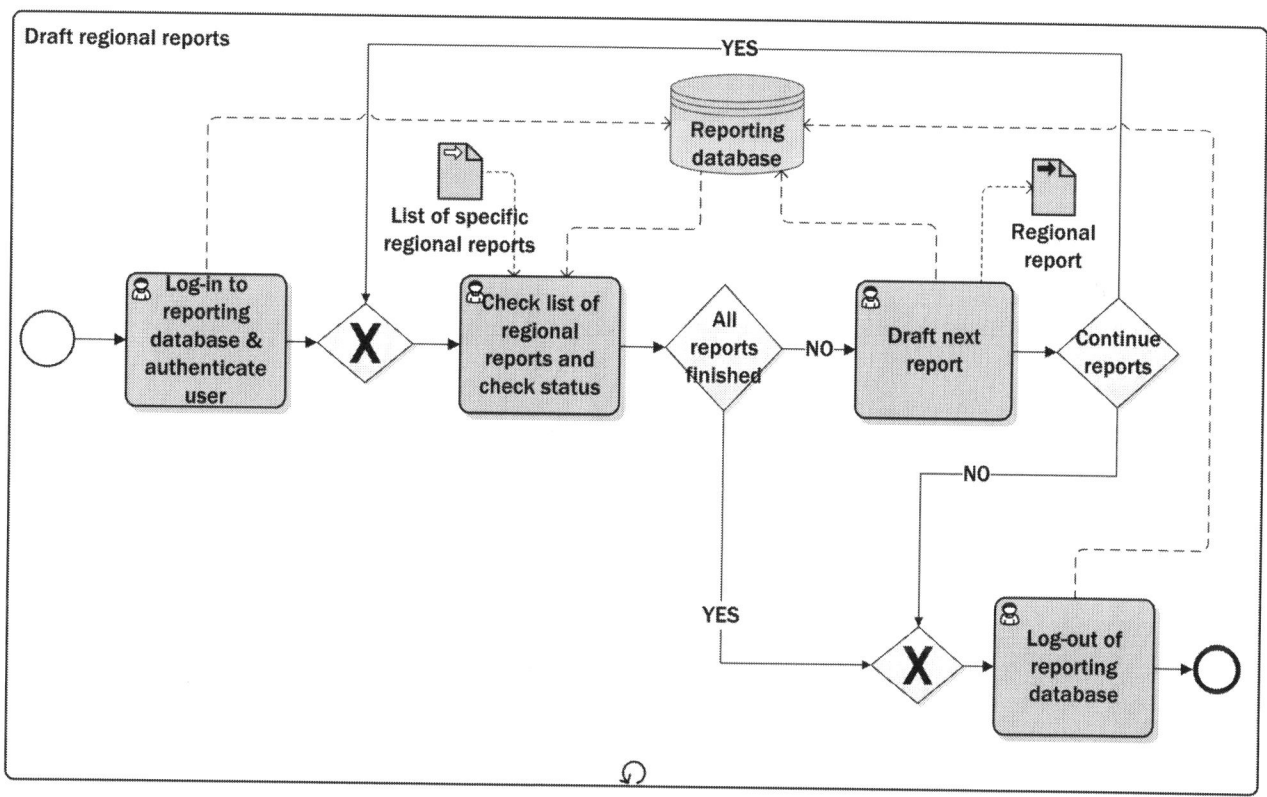

Draft regional reports

Log-in to reporting database & authenticate user

List of specific regional reports

Check list of regional reports and check status

Reporting database

All reports finished

Draft next report

Regional report

Continue reports

YES

NO

NO

YES

Log-out of reporting database

Sub-process:	**Review Reports Make Changes And Adjustments**

1. The sub-process is triggered by
    a. Country reports drafted
    b. Regional reports ready
    c. Priority report changes
    d. Country report changes ready
2. Log-in to the reporting database and download report and review
3. The country report is checked and if necessary, changes are made
4. If HQ has made changes to a priority report, the report is adjusted or published
5. If the country report needs changes, the changes and adjustments are sent to the specific country
6. Log-out of reporting database

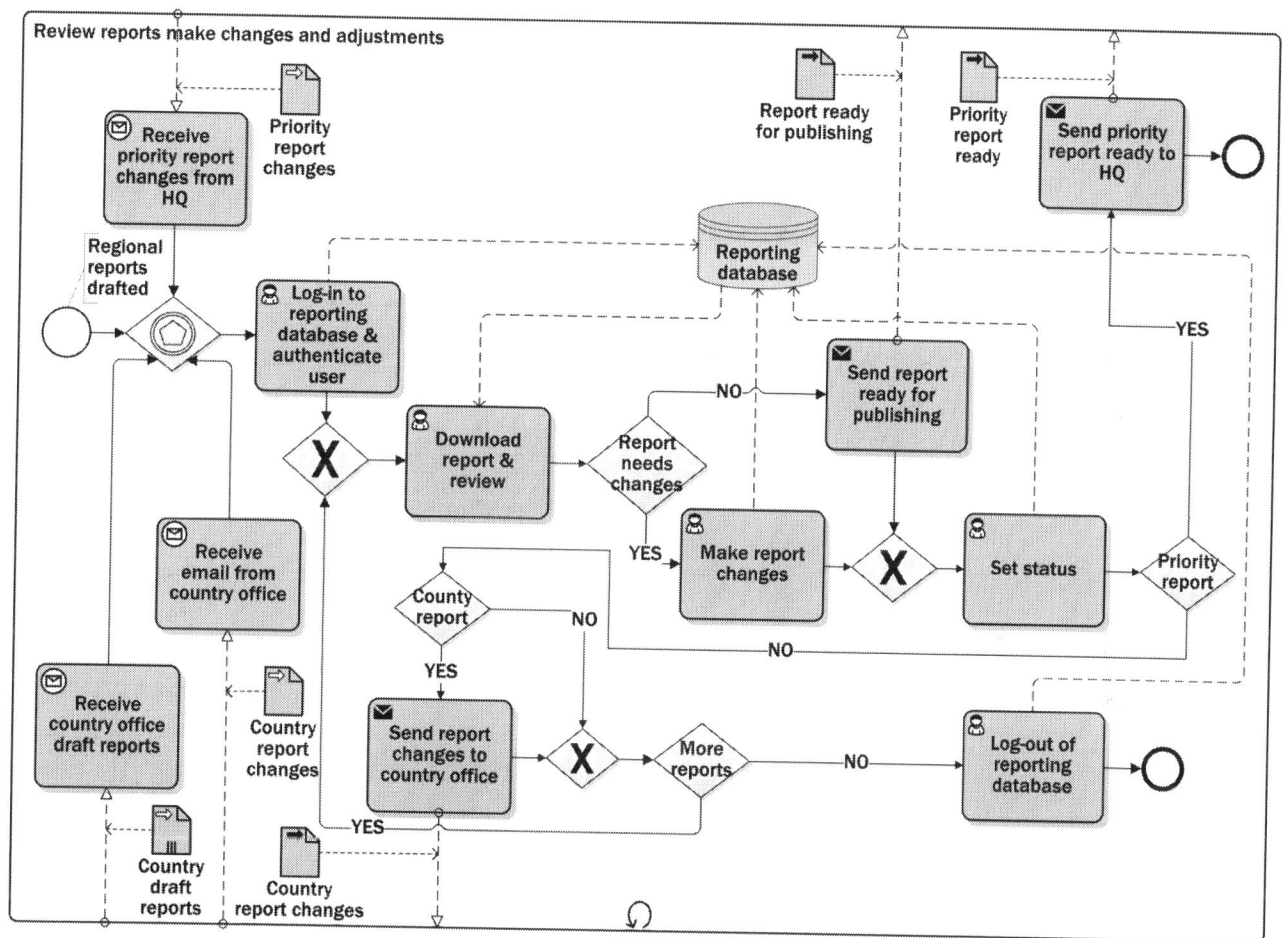

Review reports make changes and adjustments

6.3 Worldwide Annual Reporting Country Offices (CO Process)

About the process

The country office reporting is initiated by the regional office sending a list of reporting requirements. The country office allocates the required reporting and priorities. The country office sends draft reports to the regional office upon completion.

The regional office checks the report for any changes or adjustments. If adjustments are required, the report is returned to the country office. The country office makes changes with the proposed adjustments. The country office sends the changed report back to the regional office for review.

Process Collaboration

The country offices collaborate directly with their regional office.

1. The reporting is initiated by the regional office

2. Country offices allocate reporters

3. Country offices draft reports

4. Countries complete reports and inform the regional office

5. Regional office reviews the reports and either makes changes and adjustments or sends the reports for publishing

6. Country offices review report changes and make adjustments

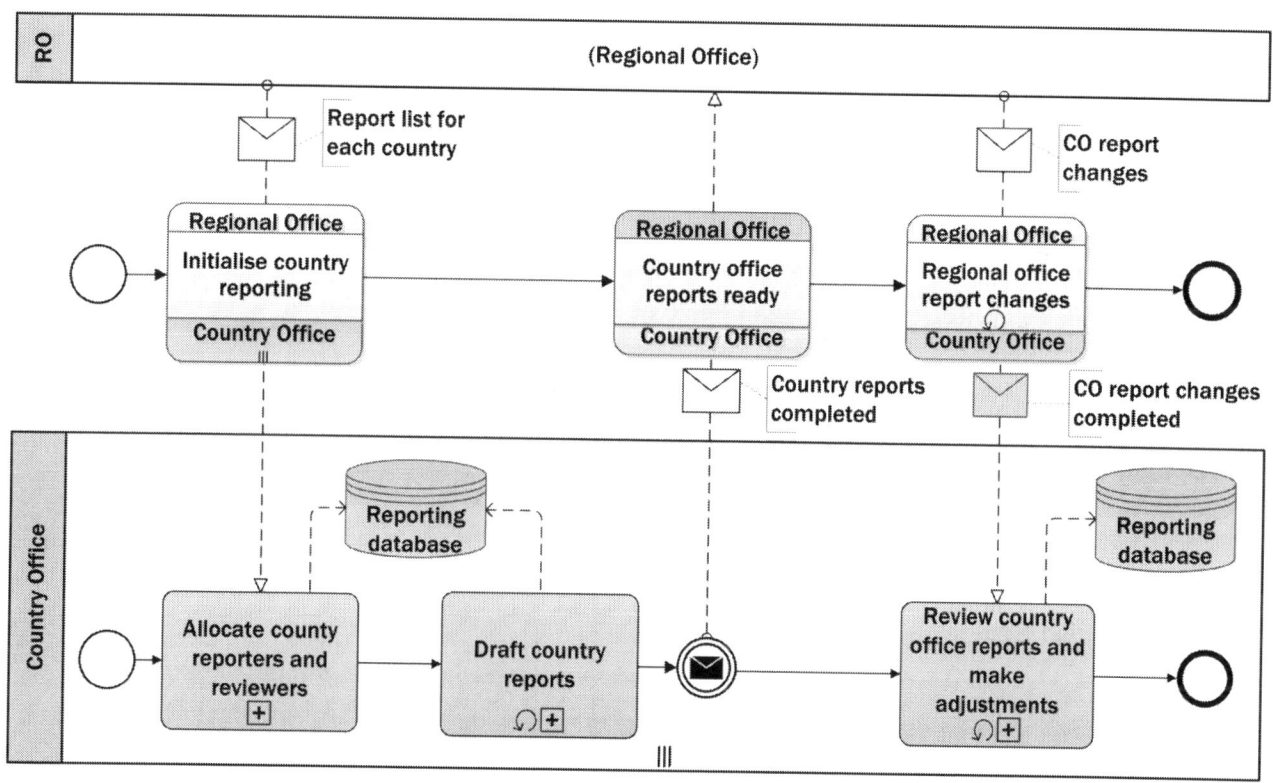

Sub-process:	**Allocate Country Reporters And Reviewers**

1. Receive country reports list

2. Check reports list

3. Log-in to the reporting database

4. Allocate staff to specific reports

5. Set report priorities

6. Log-out of reporting database

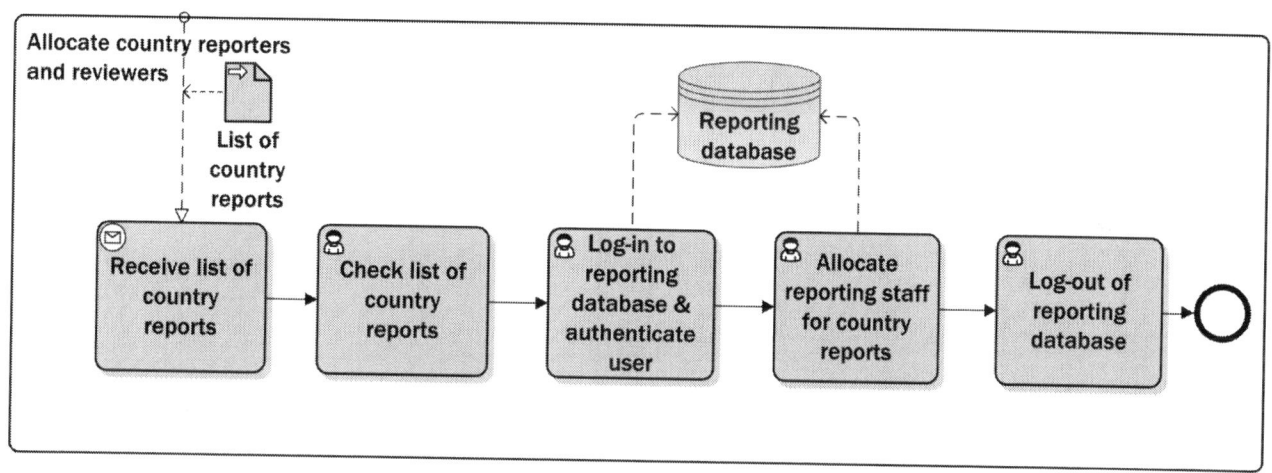

Allocate country reporters and reviewers

List of country reports

Reporting database

Receive list of country reports

Check list of country reports

Log-in to reporting database & authenticate user

Allocate reporting staff for country reports

Log-out of reporting database

Sub-process: Draft Country Reports

1. Log-in to the reporting database
2. The report list and the reporting status is checked
3. Reports are drafted
4. When all reports are completed an email is produced and sent to the regional office
5. Log-out of reporting database
6. Sub-process loops until all country reports are drafted

Admaks Publishing - BPMN Process Examples

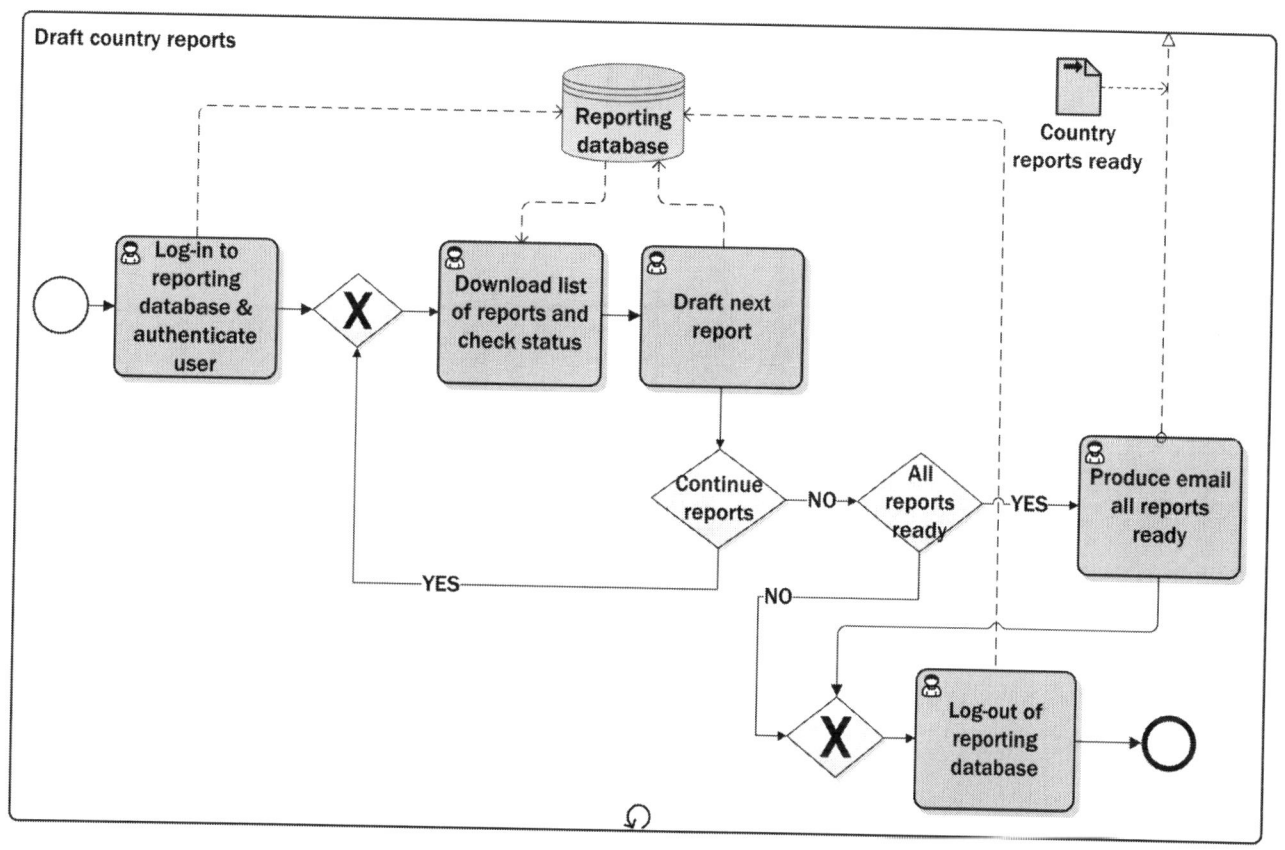

Draft country reports

Sub-process:	**Review Country Office Reports And Make Adjustments**

1. The sub-process is triggered when a country report needs changes

2. Log-in to the reporting database

3. The report is downloaded, reviewed and adjustments made

4. The status is set

5. A message is sent to the regional office informing changes have been made

6. Log-out of reporting database

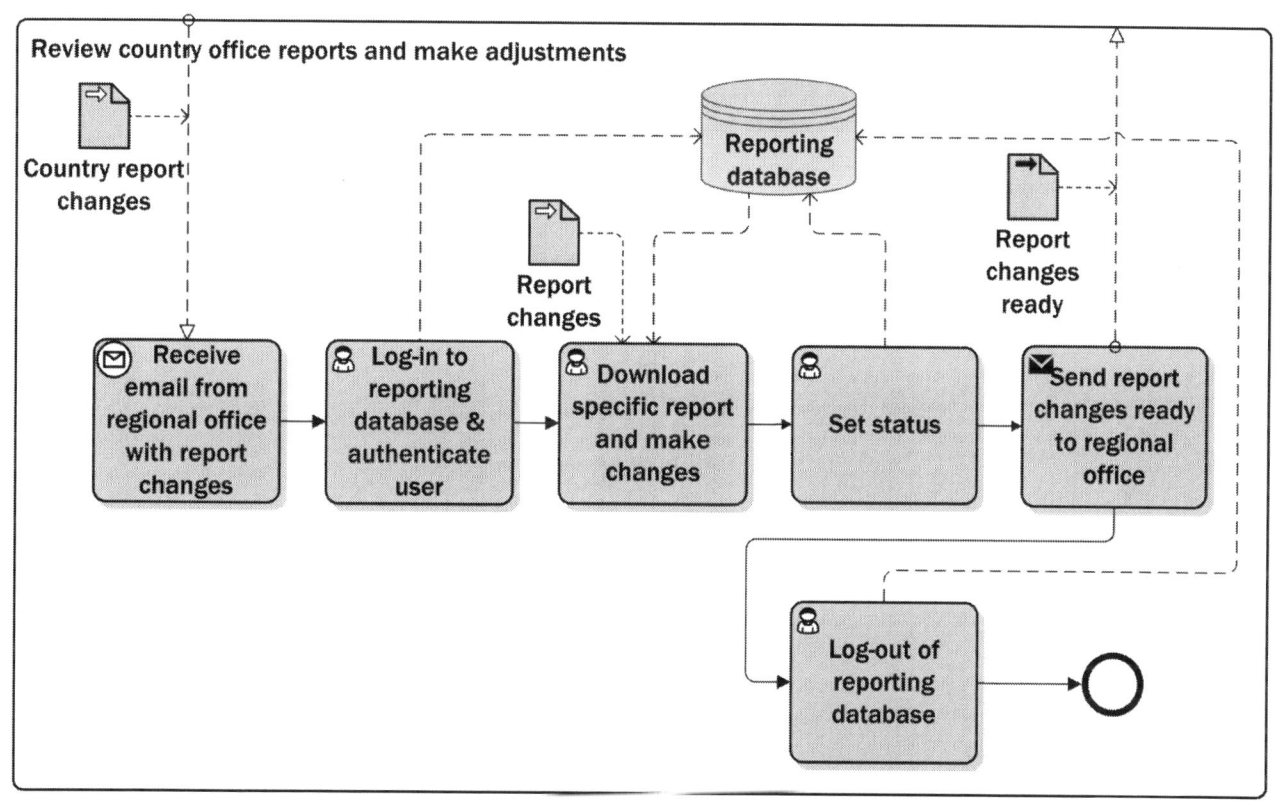

Review country office reports and make adjustments

Country report changes

Reporting database

Report changes

Report changes ready

Receive email from regional office with report changes

Log-in to reporting database & authenticate user

Download specific report and make changes

Set status

Send report changes ready to regional office

Log-out of reporting database

Process 6 Alternative Modelling Techniques

6.1   The complete overview could be one BPD i.e. HQ, Regional office and Country Office. The diagram is large but could be produced in a larger format and include all three choreography sequence flows.

6.2   In the **Country office overview,** the **Country reports completed** message could be connected to the **Draft country reports** sub-process, instead of using a message intermediate throwing event.

6.3   The **Publish reports** sub-process is a looping sub-process with two different variations. All the HQ reports are published at one time and the regional/country reports can be received at different times. An annotation describing the looping expression could be added to define the sub-process more clearly.

6.4   The sub-process **HQ review reports make changes and adjustments,** is controlled by the number of reports to be published, this is not shown in the BPD.

6.5   The looping criteria of the sub-process **Regional reports are reviewed and adjusted,** is complex. Either a good annotation could be added or it could be split into at least 2 sub-processes to include the choreography changes.

ABOUT THE AUTHOR

Since 2004 Kenneth has worked as a business process analyst using all versions of BPMN. This is his sixth book which he has written about business processes. BPMN Process Examples reveals his continuing practical and modern approach.

Kenneth gained his BPM experience working for such diverse organisations as the United Nations, UK Ministry of Defence, European Commission organisations, European Patent Office, freight companies and web service companies.

Working for these organisations has given him many years of international experience which has enabled Kenneth to diversify into teaching, giving courses and supporting companies on BPM applications. Kenneth gives workshops on business process modelling using BPMN and seminars on different BPM subjects.

FURTHER BOOKS BY THE AUTHOR

Complete BPMN Pocket Reference - ISBN 9781507546475

A practical user guide to the complete BPMN specification referencing each notation as described in Version 2.0 specification. This is a further addition to the original BPMN Pocket Reference and includes further diagrams and extended to include the complete specification 2.0.2. Business Process Diagrams are used in multiple examples to explain and demonstrate the use of the notations in a clear and concise manor.

The book is organised to enable the reader to find the notations quickly and easily and is divided into 25 chapters:

Activity Notations, Task Types, Call Activities, Event Sub-Processes, Pools and Swimlanes, Connectors, Artefacts, Messages and Conversations, Choreography, Sub-choreography, Choreography Sequence Flows, Gateways, Event Gateways, None Events, Message Events, Timer Events, Conditional Events, Multiple Events, Parallel Multiple Events, Error Events, Cancel and Terminate Events, Escalation Events, Signal Events, Compensation Events and Link Events.

Business Process Collaboration - ISBN 978-1494400217

Business Process Collaboration is a course book specifically written for those who are interested in extending their knowledge of business process modelling. This book assumes the reader has a basic knowledge of business process modelling using BPMN specification version 2.0. The BPMN latest version 2.0.1 released September 2013 has been taken into account.

This course book includes diagrams, descriptions and covers all aspects of business process collaboration. It also includes question time and student exercises with answers.

Business Process Modelling with BPMN ISBN 9781479118052

This is a course book designed for newcomers to business process modelling.

The BPMN course book has been specifically written for those who are interested in learning BPMN, its method and application, in today's business environment. This is a comprehensive course book covering all aspects of the BPMN specification.

Each BPMN notation is explained at length using examples, diagrams and descriptions. The book shows the reader how to model a simple process through to modelling and documenting the more complex business processes.

BPMN Pocket Reference - ISBN 9781470067830

This book was developed from the BPMN specification as a notation reference book. The BPMN Pocket Reference is a guide to each BPMN notation as described in the Version 2.0 specification.

The individual notations are described clearly using individual graphical diagrams showing how they are depicted. Each notation is explained with a brief description and examples of use. Notations can be easily referenced by the detailed table of contents giving the exact page of the notation and examples.

Insight into Business Processes ISBN 9783000355677

This book is a guide to business processes for those who are seeking an insight into the complex challenges of the 21st Century. The book gives a comprehensive overview and is a practical guide to business processes. It is written in an easily understandable format with clear and concise diagrams.

www.admaks.com

kenneth@admaks.com

Printed in Great Britain
by Amazon